How to Play the Harmonica for Beginners

The Ultimate Guide to Learning, Playing, and Becoming Proficient at the Instrument

Table of Contents

Introduction

Over the last decade or two, the harmonica has grown in popularity. It is perhaps the most unique member of the wind family of instruments, producing a wonderful sound with some stunning melodies. It compliments a variety of tones because it is so versatile. These genres include blues, jazz, pop, rock, and classical music, among many others.

If you are looking for something different to learn, you cannot go wrong with the harmonica. It is easy to learn, even for beginners and those who have never tried to play a musical instrument in their lives!

This book aims to walk you through all you need to know as a beginner. You'll learn how to choose the right harmonica for you, step-by-step instructions on how to hold your harmonica correctly, breathing techniques and exercises, and lots of information on notes, chords, and techniques to help you play. You'll also get plenty of practical experience, too.

Practice

As with anything, perfection can only be achieved with practice, but rather than spending one or two hours practicing once a week, try to practice daily for shorter periods of time. While it may seem easy to learn the basics, plenty of advanced techniques will take time to master – but master them you must if you are to take your harmonica playing to the next level.

It is recommended that you practice several times a week for 15 to 20 minutes at a time – daily is ideal, but as a minimum, at least three to four times a week. The more you practice, the better you will get, so build time into your weekly schedule.

With that said, it's time to dive in, and we'll start with some of the theories behind the harmonica.

Chapter 1: Understanding the Harmonica

We've all heard the haunting sound of a harmonica being played. It conjures up images of Bob Dylan, cowboys gathered around their campfire at night, and the wailing sound of the blues. If you've ever watched Breakfast at Tiffany's, you'll remember the song, Moon River, with its harmonic melody. Or perhaps you love to listen to the harmonica sounds of Billy Joel's Piano Man.

The harmonica features in music the world over, with its appealing, beautiful timbre strong enough to make itself heard over much bigger instruments. It's been used as a sideman, accompanist, and soloist and, played amplified or acoustic, it has its own classical concertos, despite being written off as a toy by many people.

Among all the other musical instruments, the harmonica is one of the smallest and most versatile and is now the instrument of choice for traveling musicians. Whether you can play any other instrument or this is your first time, the harmonica will bring challenges coupled with great pleasure.

1. *The harmonica features in music the world over. Source:*
https://pixabay.com/photos/harmonica-music-notes-book-
2619860/

The Harmonica and Its History

Several thousand years ago, the sheng, a Chinese instrument from which the harmonica originated, was first played. Because it was made of bamboo reeds, it swiftly ascended to the top of the list of instruments used in traditional Asian music. When the Sheng was introduced to Europe at the end of the 18th century, its acceptance virtually exploded overnight.

As the 19th century dawned, instrument designers began experimenting by replacing bamboo reeds with metal ones. "The Aura" was constructed in 1820 by a young instrument maker by the name of Christian Friedrich Buschmann. He employed steel reeds. Despite being mostly employed for blow notes, it did gain popularity.

The modern harmonica was invented in 1825 by Richter, a European. It contained two reed plates with 10 holes each, each of which had two metal reeds. On the other hand, the draw note could make a note when the player inhaled, whereas the first could produce a note when blown. Richter chose tones that are reminiscent of those used on diatonic harmonicas today.

In Vienna in 1829, the first mass-produced harmonicas were created, and other cities quickly followed. In the German town of Trossingen, Christian Messer and his cousin Christian Weiss began manufacturing harmonicas. They repaired the devices in their leisure time because they were also clockmakers, and they soon had a successful business on their hands. Matthias Hohner visited the cousins a few years later to learn how to make harmonicas. Hohner was a Trossingen clockmaker who founded his own harmonica business as well.

Hohner played the harmonica poorly, but his business sense was unrivaled. He was so prosperous that he acquired his rivals in 1862 and began exporting to the USA. His business kept expanding, and soon, the USA was his largest market. In 1900, he transferred the business to his sons.

Throughout the first half of the 20th century, the harmonica's appeal grew, and groups with numerous members of the instrument began to form. Hohner also invented the Chromatic harmonica, on which he placed a button on the side so that all the notes could be played. Larry Adler was the world's most well-known Chromatic harmonica musician until he passed away in 2001.

Playing the Blues

In the USA, the harmonica gained popularity as a blues instrument, and John Lee "Sonny Boy" Williamson rose to fame between the 1930s and the beginning of the 1940s. After the Second World War, Chicago rose to prominence as one of the blues music's hotbeds, giving rise to well-known artists like Little Walter and Rice Miller. Little Walter is regarded as the greatest blues player in history, and harmonica players all around the world mourned his passing in 1968.

Although Bob Dylan first made folk music popular in the 1960s, the harmonica is most frequently associated with blues music. By expanding on the past, great performers like Kim Wilson, Rod Piazza, and others from more recent times continued the blues legacy. As a result of players like Jaxon Ricci and John Popper, the introduction of consistently intriguing new styles has also grown.

In the past, many of the greatest harmonica players were Americans. The internet has helped it gain popularity, and now we can see a new generation of harmonica players from all around the world.

Types of Harmonicas

Although there are many different harmonica varieties, you will probably play with three of them:

Diatonic Harmonica

2. *The blues harp is typically used for country, folk, rock, pop, and blues music. Source: CatalpaSpirit, CC BY-SA 4.0 <https://creativecommons.org/licenses/by-sa/4.0>, via Wikimedia Commons: https://commons.wikimedia.org/wiki/File:Blues_Harp,_MS-Series,_Hohner.jpg*

Better known as a blues harp, the diatonic harmonica has 10 holes and 12 basic keys. The notes are the simple major scale, and this type of harmonica is the easiest to learn to play, making it the best for beginners.

The diatonic's major focus is on a single key: C. The key is a root note and chord that everything else revolves around musically. If you are struggling to understand the significance of the C key, imagine a piano with no black keys, only white ones.

Diatonic harmonicas are typically used for country, folk, rock, pop, and blues music.

Chromatic Harmonica

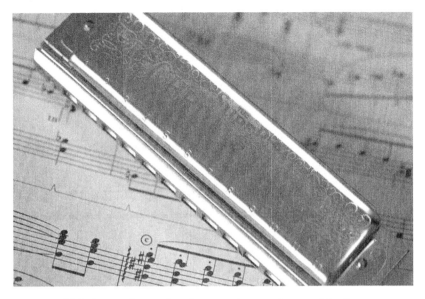

2. *This is not the easiest harmonica to play and isn't considered suitable for beginners. Source: https://pixabay.com/photos/macro-mouth-organ-harmonica-5154177/*

The chromatic harmonica may be played in all keys instead of the diatonic harmonica's focus on just one, although you can play all scales through a technique called bending. This enables players to play full scales in any key, such as major, minor, blues, pentatonic, etc., on a single instrument.

Although these harmonicas come in a choice of 10, 12, 14, and 16 holes, the most common is 12 holes. Each hole has two reeds, one for the blow note and one for the draw note.

This is not the easiest harmonica to play and isn't considered suitable for beginners. However, once you have learned to play a diatonic harmonica, you can move on to a chromatic harmonica.

With their side sliding buttons, chromatic harmonicas are usually used in jazz and classical music.

Tremolo Harmonica

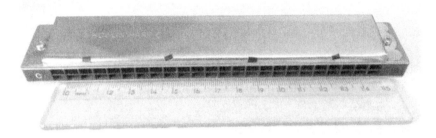

3. *Tremolo harmonicas are less complicated then chromatic and diatonic harmonicas. Source: Yves Furusho, CC BY-SA 4.0 <https://creativecommons.org/licenses/by-sa/4.0>, via Wikimedia Commons: https://commons.wikimedia.org/wiki/File:Tremolo_Harmonica_S tagg_Key_C.png*

Some claim that the tremolo harmonica is by far the easiest to learn, partly because less technical knowledge is required than the other two options.

Tremolo harmonicas have just two reeds per hole, both vibrating together when notes are blown or drawn, making them sound different from chromatic and diatonic harmonicas. However, they are limited in what you can play on them. Genres like the blues require note bending and other techniques, which you can't do with the tremolo. This limits you to simple melodies.

Like all instruments, you need to understand how it works before you can learn to play it.

Parts of a Harmonica

No matter which type of harmonica you play, they all comprise the same basic parts:

1. The Comb

All harmonicas are built around the comb, a piece in the center between the reed plates. Originally, the comb was made from wood, but plastic and metal have since replaced this. The name comes from the fact that its channels are divided in a way that makes it look like a comb. Assembled correctly, the comb and reeds form air chambers.

Reeds are flat, long strips usually made from bronze, brass, or stainless steel, and they provide space for air passage. When you blow into your harmonica, you blow air into it, and the reed alternates between blocking and unblocking the airways, vibrating to produce that unique sound.

2. Reed Plates

The reed plates are usually constructed from brass plates and are flat, square plates with one slot for each reed. The reeds are usually welded or riveted to the plate, which is screwed or nailed to the comb. Examine your harmonica, and you should see the screws right at the edge of the instrument.

Most of the time, the reed plates are screwed on, preventing the air you blow in from getting out. The blow reeds are often located on the top reed plate, while the draw reeds are typically located on the bottom reed plate.

3. Cover Plates

The name gives this one away – cover plates shield the comb and reed plates. They are usually constructed from metal, although they are wooden or plastic in some harmonicas. This usually depends on your harmonica's sound quality – the cover plates determine tonal quality.

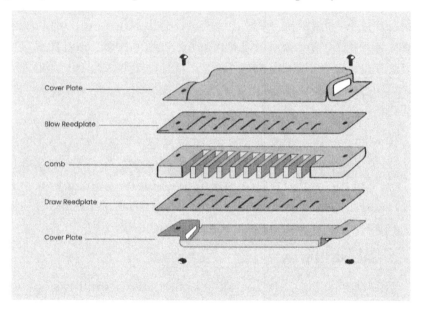

4. *All harmonicas are built around the comb, a piece in the center between the reed plates. Source: https://www.harmonica.com/wp-content/uploads/2022/02/Harmonica-Components-1024x669.png*

4. Wind savers

These are small strips of plastic, Teflon, knit paper, or leather glued to the reed plate so they lay over the reeds. You know that the harmonica is a wind instrument, so air will inevitably leak. The wind savers stop air from being lost through inactive reeds and direct air to the reed it needs.

5. Mouthpiece

When you look at your harmonica, you will see holes running right to left. These holes are air chambers, and they are in the harmonica's mouthpiece. The mouthpiece ensures the harmonica is comfortable to play and also provides the chromatic harmonica with a groove.

Before we move on, let's look at some common terms and definitions you will hear in relation to the harmonica.

Basic Harmonica Definitions

These are some of the most common terms you will hear:

- **Bend:** When the natural pitch of a reed is lowered using certain techniques. On a chromatic harmonica, all holes that have wind savers can bend in both draw and blow; typically, this means all holes except for the higher octaves (hole 8 to 12), which can only draw bend on hole 8-11, and blow bend on hole 12. On a diatonic harmonica, hole 1-6 can draw bend, and hole 7-10 can blow bend.

- **Blow:** These are sounds that are made when you breathe out. These sounds are produced by the opening of the upper reeds inside the instrument.

- **Chamber:** The region that the reeds vibrate into inside the comb. To play the instrument, you breathe into the chambers' outside holes.

- **Chromatic:** A kind of harmonica that utilizes every note found in Western music on a single instrument.

To help adjust the reed so that all notes can be played, they contain a slider button on the side.

- **Comb:** The part of the harp's center where the reed plates are placed. The comb is typically constructed of wood, plastic, or metal and has chambers or holes that you play into.

- **Covers:** These are the parts of the instrument that are joined to the comb and are also referred to as cover plates.

- **Cup:** The seal a player creates with their hands, harp, and harmonica.

- **Diatonic:** A harmonica with 10 holes, each with 2 notes, generally tuned to a Major scale.

- **Discrete:** A specific kind of diatonic harmonic comb with individual chambers for blow and draw reeds.

- **Draw:** When the player inhales, or "draws", the bottom reeds of the harmonica open, producing the "draw note".

- **Gap:** The distance between each reed and the corresponding hole in the reed plate.

- **Embouchure:** The method of using the lips, teeth and tongue to play the harmonica and is frequently used to describe a method of controlling the airflow.

- **Harp:** The harmonica goes by another name. It is also known as the "Mouth Harp," "Mouth Organ," "Short Harp," "Mississippi Saxophone," and "Tin Sandwich," and its name, "French Harp," may be an early derivation.

- **Overblow:** This happens when the player quickly switches from a draw to a blow note, choking the blow reed and only allowing the blow note to go through the draw reed. A conventional bend lowers the pitch of a natural note, whereas the overblows raise it. It is possible to overblow and bend every hole on the harmonica.

- **Position:** This is how players describe the way they play different scales on certain harmonicas. For example, the third position is playing in the key of D on a harmonica tuned to C.

- **Reed**: A narrow strip fastened to the reed plate using screws or welding. When a harmonica player inhales or exhales, these, typically constructed of metal, are triggered and spring through their slot backward or forwards, slicing the airstream and producing the sound.

- **Reed Plate:** The mounting plate for the reeds, which are paired, is typically made of brass.

- **Resonance:** Amplification of certain audible frequencies by the superimposition and echo of sound waves.

- **Slot:** A rectangular hole, slightly larger than the reed, punched in the reed plate. This is the opening through which the reed vibrates to create the sound.

- **Tab:** A note's recommended playing technique is shown in this shortened form of tablature. This differs from standard music notation, which instructs you on which note to play and for how long.

- **Tremolo** is the variation in the amplitude (volume).

- **Vibrato:** A variation in the pitch. Tremolo and vibrato are frequently combined to produce an oscillation effect in the notes. Singers typically utilize this method.

Now you understand the basics, it's time to look at how to choose the right harmonica.

Chapter 2: Choosing the Right Harmonica

Harmonicas come in all sizes, types, makes, and keys, and some of the more popular are diatonic, chromatic, and tremolo. Choosing the right one isn't easy, but for a beginner, it is recommended that you start with a 10-hole diatonic in C key. However, you should NOT choose the cheapest one you see; go for quality. The better the quality, the more reliable it will be. Let's have a look at some of the popular types.

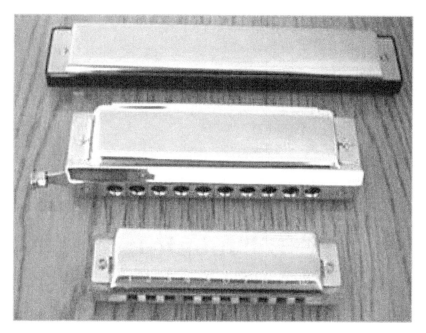

5. *Harmonicas come in all sizes, types, makes, and keys and some of the more popular are diatonic, chromatic, and tremolo. Source: Babak Babali, CC BY-SA 3.0 <https://creativecommons.org/licenses/by-sa/3.0>, via Wikimedia Commons: https://commons.wikimedia.org/wiki/File:Harmonicas.jpg*

Diatonic

Also known as harps or blues harps, many professional harmonica players use these for blues, rock, country, and jazz. These harmonicas are Richter-tuned. This means they have 19 notes. Most beginner's books are written for the C harmonica, and if you listen to beginner CDs or DVDs, they will also be played in the C key.

These are also easier to repair. If your reed plate needs replacing, it is relatively easy to do and cheaper than buying a new harmonica.

Chromatic

Chromatic harmonicas are recommended for more experienced players. Although it has the same number of reeds as a regular harmonica, the button slider makes it different. They can access the entire spectrum of notes—including flats and sharps—thanks to their slider.

Typically, these harmonicas allow you to play much more of a song's main melody than a diatonic harmonica does, and they are often used in blues. However, because they are so versatile, they are well suited to many genres, including classical, soul, pop, and jazz. Experienced players can play virtually all genres on a chromatic harmonica.

Solo-Tuned

These are excellent for solos and melodies because they supply all the harmonica's scale notes across their entire octave range. In terms of use, they are much the same as the chromatic harmonica and are good for Irish, classical, rock, jazz, blues, and pop music.

Choosing a Harmonica Based on Music Style

You can also pick your harmonica based on the style of music you want to play. Here's a quick guide:

Irish and Scottish Folk Music

Diatonic:

The most popular diatonic harmonica for jigs, reels, and other similar Irish folk music styles is one tuned in the G key. These music styles are best played with well-tuned, airtight, responsive harmonica. Diatonics tuned in the A key are more popular in Scottish folk music. The top models are readily available off the shelf and contain metal or plastic combs. The top models are:

- Cross Harp
- Golden Melody
- Hering Blues & Black Blues
- Lee Oskar by Tombo
- Meisterclass
- Seydel
- Suzuki Pro Master

Tremolo:

Tremolos are frequently employed in Irish music due to their lovely accordion-like sound. They are typically tuned in a 3-octave range, for example, just like a diatonic harp. The octaves, in this instance, are as follows:

- **First Octave:** DO RE MI SO TI DO
- **Second Octave:** DO RE MI FA SO LA TI DO
- **Third Octave:** DO RE MI FA SO LA DO

However, this is kind of restrictive because many of the songs that use a D whistle would not be within the scope of a tremolo tuned in D. Bending notes is not easy on a tremolo harmonica, either. The only way to get around this is to purchase a solo-tuned or huge four-to-six-octave harmonica.

Chromatic:

If folk music is your thing, chromatic harmonicas are by far the best choice because you get a full scale, and folk music doesn't require complicated bends. That said, the chromatic and the 10-hole diatonic are two completely different beasts,

Three of the best to buy are:

- Hering
- Hohner
- Seydel

Blues Music

The diatonic harmonica is, without a doubt, the best harmonica for blues. Pick a dependable diatonic instrument from Suzuki, Lee Oskar, Seydel, Hering, or Hohner.

Pop Music, Rock and R&B

Once more, the diatonic harmonica is ideal for these. However, a chromatic harmonica may occasionally work as well.

Classical Music

Choose a good quality chromatic harmonica made by Seydel, Hohner, Suzuki, or Hering.

Jazz Music

Jazz benefits most from chromatics, while diatonic can occasionally be used.

Understanding Harmonica Keys and Positions

Now, we get to the complicated bit. Choosing the right harmonica requires that you know which keys you want, and this is where things get a little confusing because you also need to understand harmonica positions. This chapter will discuss the common positions and how to decide on the best one to use. We'll also look briefly at alternative tunings and overblowing.

Harmonica Positions

Occasionally, you may hear a harmonica player saying things that make it sound like they are speaking a foreign language. Those things include:

- Cross harp
- 5th position
- Straight harp

Unless you have any background in harmonica positions, you will not understand what these mean – yet. Players explain how various scales are performed on a harmonica using these terms, which are no more sophisticated than playing positions.

Given that the diatonic harmonica comes in a variety of keys, "position" is one of the most helpful concepts to understand. The relative note placement is the same for all of them, making playing songs in multiple keys simpler because you may use the same holes when you learn a tune in one key.

Let's start with a standard C harmonica and the note layout:

HOLE	1	2	3	4	5	6	7	8	9	10
BLOW	C	E	G	C	E	G	C	E	G	C
DRAW	D	G	B	D	F	A	B	D	F	A

The C harmonica's lowest note is, as you can see from the image above, the hole 1 blow. Since C is the harmonica's natural tonic and midpoint, it is tuned in C-Major. The key of a harmonica can also be discovered in other ways. Look at the following key arrangement:

HOLE	1	2	3	4	5	6	7	8	9	10
BLOW	G	C	E	G	C	E	G	C	E	G
DRAW	B	D	G	B	D	F	A	B	D	F

As you can see, the first hole now has two additional notes, and the notes you would have expected to see on the first hole are now on the second. This harp is tuned in G, then. Because G is the lowest note on the hole 1 blow, we could infer that. Then again, look. We still have a C-Major scale and the C-blow chord. This means that the extra hole doesn't really change anything and that the harmonica is still tuned to C.

We can play songs on the harmonica in a variety of keys thanks to the different positions. 12 keys are present:

- Ab
- A
- Bb
- B
- C
- Db
- D
- Eb

- E
- F
- F#
- G

According to theory, this implies that there must be 12 harmonica positions. If you wanted to play a C harmonic in the key of C, all you had to do was start and end your scales on C.

Once more examining the aforementioned pattern, we can determine that the best places to begin a C scale are either the first, fourth, or seventh blows. The primary focal point of music is the tonic, also referred to as the C note.

To play in a different key, simply choose a different note to serve as the tonic. For instance, every scale on a harmonica tuned to C must start and conclude on G, and the first, second, third, and fourth draw notes combine to form a G chord. Next, the tonic shifts to G.

A new mode or influence results when the key is changed. First position, often known as straight harp, is the term used to describe playing the harmonica in its tuned key. Other common positions are:

- **Second Position or Cross Harp:** playing a C harp in the G key.

- **Third Position:** playing a C harp in the D key.

- **Fourth Position:** playing a C harp in the A key.

While there are other positions, they are not used so much. Let's look at the first four positions in more detail.

First Position

The first position is sometimes referred to as the Straight Harp. You are in the key that your harp is labeled for when you play in the first position. This position enables you to perform a wide range of melodies, including ragtime and folk pieces, by utilizing the expressive upper register.

Fun Fact

One of the top players in this position was Little Walter, and you can hear it used in many of his tunes.

Second Position

The Cross Harp is another name for the second position. The harp must be played seven semitones above the key it is listed in order to play the second position. The perfect fifth is how we refer to it. For instance, the G note is in the second position on a harmonica tuned to C. On this, music from the country, rock, and blues genres is commonly performed. If you want to play the low holes, 1 through 5, which are mostly draw notes, you must have a solid grasp of bending.

Fun Fact

The first person ever officially acknowledged in this function was Henry Whitter. In 1892, he was born in Fries, Virginia. The opening track on his 1923 Okeh label album was the traditional cross harp tune "Rain Crow Bill Blues."

Third Position

This is sometimes called the Slant Harp. Playing the third position on a C harmonica means playing seven semitones, or a perfect fifth, from G – that means the D key. In simple terms, the third position is played in a key two semitones over the labeled key. D is the focus, and the music is played one full step above the labeled key. The emphasis is on playing holes 4 through 6 draw, with hole 4 draw serving as the start and finish location. The third position is ideally suited for blues and folk music played in the minor key since it is highly melancholy and has a minor feel.

Fun Fact

One of the top players in this position was Little Walter, and you can hear it used in many of his tunes.

Fourth Position

The A key occupies the fourth position. Similar to the third, it has a minor vibe and works well for minor-key music. The hole 3 draw bend is where the start and end points are located. The fourth position is among the hardest because it is not a simple note to hit.

Now that you know, you can use the same harmonica to play songs in a variety of keys. But that doesn't imply you have to use the same harmonica forever or only play in one key. For instance, you could play the blues in the first position on a harmonica tuned to C. However, using an F-tuned harmonica and playing in the second position would be preferable.

Playing in the second position allows you to bend expressive notes in the lower register. Yes, you can play the blues on the harmonica in the first position. It's a crucial position for blues playing since it allows you to do a lot of things that you couldn't accomplish in other positions. The tones offered by various keys vary, and each location has its own feel and advantages. Try each one out to discover which one suits you the best.

Overbending

The notes of the diatonic scale can be played on the diatonic harmonica. These are the major scale notes on harmonicas tuned to Richter. The full scale can be played in the second octave, but some notes wouldn't be present in the first and third octaves. Here, bending is used. You can reach those notes that are lacking when you learn to bend. Despite this, you still won't have access to the whole 12-note chromatic scale that is employed in many musical genres.

Using the overblow and overdraw techniques, you can achieve the missing notes that are impossible to obtain with conventional blow and draw bending. These allow you to fully explore a diatonic harmonica's chromatic range.

Fun Fact

It is thought that James Simon, sometimes known as Blues Birdhead, created the first overblow recording when he cut "Mean Low Blues" in 1929. But it wasn't until Howard Levy that we started to fully comprehend and use these tones. His mastery of the approach brought the simple harp to new, lofty heights and opened up a new dimension in harmonica playing.

When you use the overbend technique, you can play all 12 keys on one diatonic harp and in any position.

In order to get the notes, it needs to be made clear that you don't have to blow or draw more violently while employing the overblow and overdraw processes. If your harmonica is set up correctly, you can play overbent notes just as softly as normal notes. The secret is in technique, the proper embouchure, and a lot of repetition.

Alternate Tunings

There are other ways to tune a diatonic harmonica, but Richter tuning is the most popular. The Richter tuning of the harmonica is the foundation of the majority of tunes, although it isn't always the best option for all musical styles. There are many different customized tunings that can be used to play specific musical genres more easily. Listed below are a handful of the most typically used:

Country Tuning

This is the Richter tuning with the hole 5 draw raised half a step. Here's the layout:

HOLE	1	2	3	4	5	6	7	8	9	10
BLOW	C	E	G	C	E	G	C	E	G	C
DRAW	D	G	B	D	F#	A	B	D	F	A

We can play the major 7 note without overblowing by lifting the five draw, and we also obtain a major 7 chord. When performed in the cross-harp position, this can be employed for music with a subdominant, strong chord. You can also bend the hole 5 draw, and doing so still gives you access to the dominant 7 note. This tuning's additional note is frequently employed in melodies.

Natural Minor

For minor tunes played in the first and second positions, this tuning is the finest. Here is the arrangement:

HOLE	1	2	3	4	5	6	7	8	9	10
BLOW	C	Eb	G	C	Eb	G	C	Eb	G	C
DRAW	D	G	Bb	D	F	A	Bb	D	F	A

In this tuning, the blow and draw chords are minor, as opposed to major in a traditional tuning. Playing minor songs on a harmonica with this tuning is less difficult than with a harmonica tuned to Richter.

Diminished Tuning

The layout for this tuning is as follows:

HOLE	1	2	3	4	5	6	7	8	9	10
BLOW	Eb	F#	A	C	Eb	F#	A	C	Eb	F#
DRAW	F	G#	B	D	F	G#	B	D	F	G#

With this setup, you can play all chromatic notes by just employing the bending technique. This tuning technique is known as expressive tuning because it has semitone bends on each hole. With this melody, you can play all 12 keys on a single harmonica.

Although diminished tuning is a brilliant idea, you must be an accomplished musician to grasp it. Before you can even start learning this, you must master accurate bending.

Although these are only a handful of the tunings offered, they give you a general sense of what to look for when selecting your harmonica. This was only to give you an outline of things to look for when buying your first harmonica. Most of what has been covered in this chapter is covered in more detail later.

Harmonica Positions Chart

To finish this chapter, here's a harmonica position chart and instructions on how to use it:

Key	1st Position	2nd Position	3rd Position	4th Position	5th Position	6th Position	7th Position	12th Position
G	G	D	A	E	B	F#	Db	C
Ab	Ab	Eb	Bb	F	C	G	D	Db
A	A	E	B	F#	Db	Ab	Eb	D
Bb	Bb	F	C	G	D	A	E	Eb
B	B	F#	Db	Ab	Eb	Bb	F	E
C	C	G	D	A	E	B	F#	F

Db	Db	Ab	Eb	Bb	F	C	G	F#
D	D	A	E	B	F#	Db	Ab	G
E	E	B	F#	Db	Ab	Eb	Ab	A
F	F	C	G	D	A	E	B	Bb
F#	F#	C#	Ab	Eb	Bb	F	C	B

How to Use

1. Determine your desired playing position.

2. Locate the position on the top row of the chart above.

3. Look down the column until you find the correct key.

4. Look at the first column on the left to see which harmonica key corresponds to it.

There is no need to memorize this to decide on the right harmonica key for a specific tune because there's an easier way.

Let's say you are playing a C-tuned harp and must determine the correct second-position key. Simply count five up from the harmonica key:

1. C – harmonica key

2. D, 3

3. E, 4

4. F, 5

5. G

So, playing the second position on a C-tuned harmonica is the G key.

Chapter 3: Holding and Playing Your Harmonica

Now, we get to the fun part: learning how to hold and play your harmonica correctly. Not learning the right technique is a huge mistake, and it's one that many beginners make. If you learn bad habits right at the start of your journey, your performance will suffer, and you'll struggle to unlearn them. One of those bad habits is not holding your harmonica correctly.

Most beginners pick up a harmonica and hold it how they think it should be held, in a comfortable position. Try it. It won't go well; I promise you that. Because you don't have the right grip, your notes won't sound good, you'll struggle with volume, and you will likely drop your harp a few times.

Do that, and you'll have to go back to the beginning. You'll need to unlearn what you taught yourself and relearn the right way. That's why I urge you not to pick up your harmonica without the help of this chapter.

Guide to Holding Your Harmonica Properly

Initially, these steps might not feel natural, but as you practice, you will start to see the importance of holding your harmonica in the right position as you play your notes. This is even more important when drawing notes. A good grasp of the harp will stop it from moving about too much; if it does, you'll likely play the wrong notes.

These steps have been written assuming that your dominant hand is your right hand. If it isn't, you can switch hands. As you get more comfortable playing your instrument, you'll likely adjust your position, but before you even think about that, get comfortable with these steps first.

Here we go.

Step One: Turn Your Harmonica Lengthways So the Numbers Face Up.

This is the proper upright stance. The numbers go from 1 on the left to 10 on the right when playing a diatonic harp.

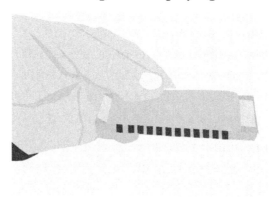

6. This is the proper upright stance. Source:
https://musicalinstrumentguide.com/wp-
content/uploads/2020/02/Harmonica-numbers-top_700x398.jpg

Step Two: Form Your Left Hand into a C-Shape and Put the Harmonica Inside.

Aim to position the side with hole number 1 as far in as possible. In order to see all the hole numbers, your fingertip should rest along the top of the harmonica and as far back as necessary. Make sure your forefinger does not touch the numbers as you grip the harmonica with your thumb along the bottom.

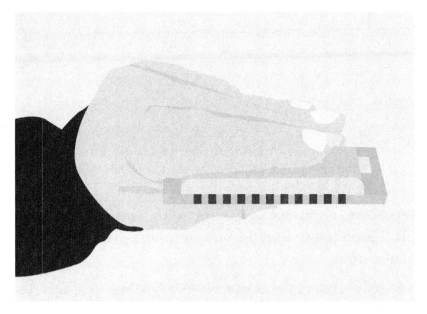

7. *Form your left hand into a C-shape and put the harmonica inside. Source: https://musicalinstrumentguide.com/wp-content/uploads/2020/02/Holding-a-harmonica-left-hand_700x364.jpg*

Step Three: Put Your Middle Finger behind the Harp.

Your left hand should now be cupped around your harmonica, with your middle finger supporting it at the back.

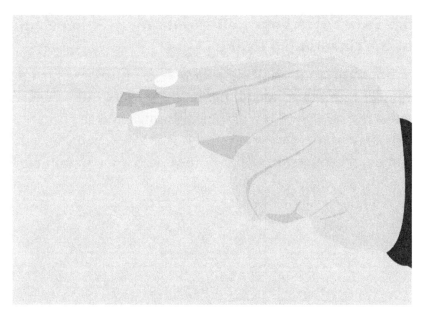

8. Put your middle finger behind the harp. Source: https://musicalinstrumentguide.com/wp-content/uploads/2020/02/Holding-harmonica-front-view_700x380.jpg

Step Four: Form a Cup Shape with Your Pinky and Left Ring Finger Facing You beneath the Harmonica.

Simply said, it produces an extra sound chamber that increases resonance when you play your harmonica.

Step Five: Place Your Right Hand beneath the Harmonica.

By placing your right thumb on the right side of the harmonica, you can support it. This prevents the harp from slipping as you play it by moving it back and forth.

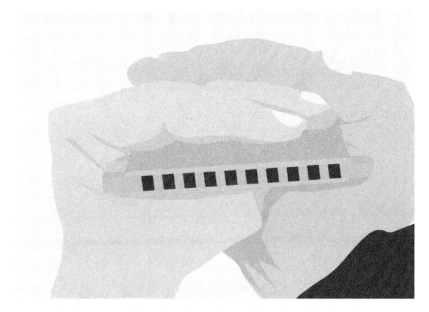

9. *By placing your right thumb on the right side of the harmonica, you can support it. Source: https://musicalinstrumentguide.com/wp-content/uploads/2020/02/Holding-harmonica-both-hands_700x400.jpg*

Step Six: Wrap Your Right Fingers Over Your Left Fingers.

By now, your grip should be closed around the harmonica but not covering the front end fully. There must not be any part of your hand covering the holes; you should be able to blow and draw on each one.

Changing Your Grip for Resonance and Tone

You can vary your grip with your dominant hand in a couple of ways. As you become better at playing, these can help you, but you should learn about them now.

- **Closed Cup = Lower Tones and Muted Effect**

When you cup your dominant hand over the front and seal with your non-dominant hand, the effect is heavy-bass or muffled. This produces a sound that is common in several musical genres, especially the blues.

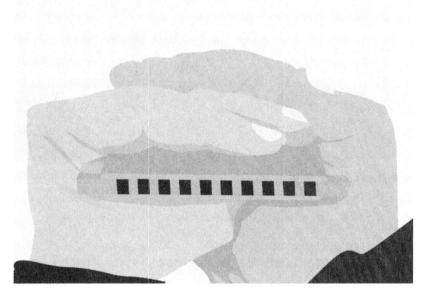

10. Closed cups produce lower tones and a muted effect. Source: https://musicalinstrumentguide.com/wp-content/uploads/2020/02/Holding-harmonica-closed-grip_700x400.jpg

- **Open Hands = Higher Tones and Better Resonance**

Higher notes and considerably better resonance can be obtained, allowing the sound to travel much farther if the fingers on both hands are drawn back to open the harmonica's front.

You may produce a wah-wah effect by switching back and forth between these two methods.

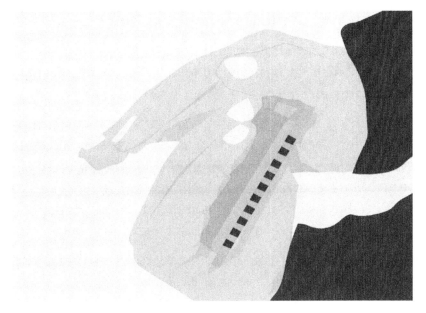

11. Open hands produce higher tones and better resonance. Source: https://musicalinstrumentguide.com/wp-content/uploads/2020/02/Harmonica-holding-open-grip_700x400.jpg

What Not to Do When Handling a Harmonica

When learning how to hold their harp and get a great sound out of it, beginners frequently make typical blunders. The errors you should avoid are as follows:

- **Playing with One Hand**

This is a sloppy, sluggish method to play, but more importantly, it will be difficult for you to transition notes rapidly. Switching between notes, managing your loudness, and producing that wah-wah effect will be much simpler if you hold the harmonica properly with both hands.

- **Looking at the Harmonica as You Play**

If you handle your harmonica properly, you won't be able to see most of it. Because you shouldn't see it while playing, it is frequently referred to as a "blind" instrument.

You may train your mouth to recognize each hole just like a typewriter learns to touch type without looking at the keyboard's keys. If you are continually looking to make sure you are doing it correctly, your technique will deteriorate. You won't need to use your eyes if you maintain the proper hold, freeing your mind to concentrate on touch and sound.

- **Not Moving the Harmonica and Moving Your Head**

Your actions will only come from your hands and tongue if you have the proper grip. Your tongue handles the remaining action as your hands back and forth the harp as necessary. You must not move your head!

- **Trying to Learn Advanced Skills without Mastering Your Grip**

Forget the wah-wah effect, vibrato, overblowing, and bending for now. To train your lips and hands to perform the task, you must first master the right grip. Train your ears to listen and learn each hole one at a time without looking away so you are not constantly gazing down.

Attempting to Multitask

You might need to adjust your grip if you're using a microphone or playing another instrument at the same time. There are several distinctions that you need to be aware of, even if the majority of the aforementioned strategies and advice still apply in this situation.

- **Playing with a Mic**

Installing the microphone on a stand is ideal if you want to amp up or record your harmonica playing without shifting your grip. Ensure that the stand is set to the mouth's height.

Make sure there is enough room between the harp and microphone so you can move your hands freely. The last thing you want is for your microphone to fall over during your performance!

If you don't have a stand, hold the microphone in your left hand while making sure to allow a few inches between it and the harp. Use the pinky and ring fingers on your left hand to hold the microphone in place. Your right hand is now free to create effects or give the microphone extra support.

- **Playing Another Instrument**

You'll need to switch things up if you wish to play the guitar or another instrument in addition to the harmonica. You will need to buy a rack or holder for the harmonica so that you can play the other instrument instead of holding the harmonica in your hands.

These holders fit around your neck and are tightened with a screw so that they can cover your mouth. Some are made of metal, while others are padded for comfort.

Contrary to what you initially learned, you will not move your hands in this situation. Your head will, though. Switching notes without moving your head too much will be simpler if you use the proper tongue techniques.

Before you even consider attempting to play two instruments simultaneously, you must acquire the proper grip because it is crucial, especially for beginners. It takes some time to become accustomed to using a harmonica holder, so start with the fundamentals.

How to Position Your Lips and Mouth

Once you have learned the correct grip, you must learn how to position your lips and mouth to play the harmonica.

1. As you hold your harmonica, open your mouth and raise the harp closer to your mouth using your forearms. Do NOT move your head, only the harp.

2. Unfold your lips, place the harmonica between them, and close them to rest gently on the cover.

3. Try blowing into it gently; listen to the sound you get. Then, inhale a breath (draw) to see what sound that produces.

That is the simple way of doing it, so now you must learn how the pros do it. Incorrect mouth positioning is common among beginners, leading to weak notes.

To avoid this, try these ideas:

1. Open your mouth like you are giving a big yawn, and push the harmonica slowly to the back of it. As you do this, make sure the mouthpiece goes past your front teeth. This ensures better access to all

the holes on the harp and makes your sound much fuller.

2. Tilt the harmonica slowly so the mouthpiece faces down. This gives you space to use the tongue-blocking technique you'll learn about later. It also takes a lot of hard work out of this technique.

3. Jerk your tongue left to right over the holes and listen to the sound it produces.

Breathing Techniques

The last thing to learn is how to breathe properly to produce full, nice-sounding notes without running out of breath.

Blows and Draws

You play each note by blowing or drawing on a hole. You can also use bending to change the pitch, but you'll learn more about that later. Blow notes are created by blowing onto the harp, while draw notes come from sucking the air out.

The most frequent but reasonable error beginning players make is thinking that blows are played by blowing into the harmonica as though blowing up a balloon, while draws are done by sucking as though smoking a cigarette or vaping. This is incorrect since it will just result in dreadful noises that you won't be able to control.

How to Breathe Properly

To learn how to play blows and draw properly, follow these steps:

- **Relaxation:** How you inhale and exhale into the harp should seem natural and consistent with how you normally breathe. Take a few deep breaths before starting.

- **Breathe from the Diaphragm:** While playing the harmonica, you should only breathe via your diaphragm, which is located slightly above your stomach. This gives you complete control and enables you to regulate your breathing. Breathing in through your nose rather than your mouth is the most straightforward way to do this. If you're not sure how deep breathing with the diaphragm should feel, do it a few times and pay attention to how your shoulders rise and fall. Your shoulders should not move during proper diaphragmatic breathing. Instead, they should remain still.

- **The Harmonica's Placement in Your Mouth:** Lick some of the harmonica's middle holes while moistening your lips. Make sure the holes in the harmonica are just in front of your teeth and just past your lips as you place them in your mouth. If you're holding the harmonica correctly, your lips should rest on the cover and gently touch your left fingers. Usually, the longer you can hold it in your mouth while still breathing normally, the better tone you will generate. Make sure your cup is halfway open and that your hands are properly positioned.

- **Lower Your Bottom Jaw:** Keep your mouth in the same position, but gently lower your jaw to create more room for resonance. This makes your tone better.

- **Take a Few Breaths:** Breathe normally into the holes towards the middle of the comb, making sure the harmonica is in the proper position in your mouth. Keep going until everything comes naturally to you.

Make sure your posture is correct when you do this. Do not slouch. Sit up straight and keep your shoulders back. The more often you do something, the more at ease you'll feel doing it.

How to Build Endurance

You'll probably get out of breath rather quickly when you first start practicing your breathing techniques. Additionally, you can feel cracked lips and a dry mouth. Be at ease; these are very typical. Harmonica playing puts a lot of stress on the respiratory system, and until your body adjusts, you'll experience breathlessness rather rapidly. By taking your time and building up gradually, you can get through this. For a week, practice the proper breathing for five minutes each day. The following week, five more minutes every day, and so forth. Your body will eventually adjust, and your endurance will increase.

When you breathe deeply and gently through a large space with no leaks or obstacles, your harmonica playing will be at its optimum. You can practice the breathing techniques listed below.

Big Yawns

Yawning is incredibly catching – you yawn, and everyone else around you starts yawning! Try a big yawn now and see what happens. You should be aware that the air can freely move through your lips and throat. You feel at ease when the yawn comes to an end.

The fat pipe is what you might refer to as the free flow of oxygen with an open neck. There is nothing to get in the way of the air moving about pleasantly. Sound waves enter your lungs and begin to resonate at the same time.

Air can move silently when you breathe slowly and with your neck open. If you can hear the air when you breathe, try a yawn to open your mouth and keep it open to allow the air to pass freely and silently.

Of course, you can't play the harmonica with your mouth open, so yawn in your throat with your lips just a finger's breadth apart.

The Balloon Exercise

When playing, if any air does not go through your harmonica, it is considered leakage. This produces a weaker sound and weakens your endurance. The air that enters your nose is a part of this. You can attempt this exercise if you have trouble stopping the airflow via your nose.

You don't use a balloon for this, despite the name. You will pretend to blow one up instead. Blow like you are inflating a balloon by pressing your lips on the back of your palm. If you have a good seal, the air won't escape. Therefore, your cheeks should swell up. Next, try sucking in your cheeks as you inhale. If you can accomplish this, you can play the harmonica while keeping your nose shut. Put this into regular practice.

The Warm Hand Exercise

Because the reeds in your harmonica are small, heavy breathing is not required to make a sound. Honestly, you don't need a lot of breath to get the reeds to vibrate. You may learn how delicate that breath needs to be by practicing the warm hand technique.

Hold out your hand with the palm up. Bring it up to your mouth, stopping about two fingers' breadth away. You can feel warm air blowing over your palm when you softly inhale, but you cannot feel the air itself. Breathe on it. Inhale now. The whole goal of this exercise is to practice slowly exhaling and inhaling, so use your imagination.

Perform this practice before playing your harmonica until you have more experience. Once you have the breathing down, experiment with the same airflow.

Deep Breathing

You'll find out more about the air column that each of us has later. For the time being, realize that it extends from your lips to the base of your lungs. Your voice is amplified, and the air in your lungs is used to gently manipulate your harp when the entire column moves. Here's how it's done:

1. Face a far-off horizon; you'll have to visualize it while sitting or standing straight.

2. Take a calm, gentle breath in, feeling your rib cage and abdomen expand.

3. Gently exhale while drawing your belly button in. Make sure your ribcage and shoulders are stretched as you do this. Don't let your ribs stiffen up.

Maintain consistent, deep breathing. Relax your shoulders, open your chest, and breathe from your abdomen. Pay close attention to your breathing as you do this:

1. All the work must be done by your abdomen. Your abdomen should swell as you inhale and contract when you exhale. Your lungs will be filled with oxygen as a result of taking slow, deep breaths like this, which will give the harmonica sound plenty of room to vibrate. Your shoulders and ribcage shouldn't move significantly, so avoid doing so. You use less effort and may move more quickly when your abdomen does the work.

2. Maintain steady breathing to maintain airflow. The intensity of each breath should be consistent throughout. Try not to breathe in sharp bursts as you begin a fresh breath. Starting the note and continuing to breathe until you need to play the next one is how to get the best note out of a harmonica.

Breathe deeply and slowly so you can feel the air moving around you. Take note of how breathing makes you feel. Try to inhale for at least three seconds and exhale for exactly the same amount of time. It will only work if your breath is calm for a longer period of time. If you find it difficult to maintain the full three seconds, try for two seconds with a smaller air volume and progressively increase.

The Devious Laugh Exercise

Have you ever listened to an evil genius from a cartoon or movie laugh? Then you'll know that they know exactly how to use their diaphragm. This is the muscle that pushes you through deep breathing, and you can use that same power to make your harmonica sound much richer. Deepen your breathing with these steps.

1. Put your hands on your stomach and loudly exclaim, "Hah!" Repetition is required. Observe how the sound makes your abdomen bounce out; that is your diaphragm at work, expelling air from your lungs.

2. At this point, take a sharp breath in as though someone or something just startled you. As the air in your lungs fills up, you'll notice that your diaphragm immediately tightens, pulling inward.

Put some oomph into your harmonica sound by using these thrusts.

Regular breathing exercises will help you produce a harmonica sound that sounds significantly different.

It's time to move on to the really exciting part, which is learning some methods to improve your harmonica playing.

Chapter 4: Mastering Single Notes and Tongue Blocking

The harmonica is an incredible instrument. It may be small, but it is powerful and unique in many ways. One of the ways is that playing two or three notes is far easier than playing one. You need to learn certain techniques to isolate notes, and we'll talk about those shortly.

Techniques for Single Notes

When you blow into your harmonica for the first time, you will likely get two or more notes playing simultaneously. You must learn to play each note individually to understand what single notes sound like. Choose one hole in the harp and block off the holes on either side using your fingers. Blow into that hole, and a single note will play.

You can use two techniques to get single notes:

- Tongue blocking.
- Lip pursing or puckering.

As puckering is the easiest for beginners, we'll start with that using a basic technique.

1. Choose any note on the harmonica, for example, hole 4 blow.

2. Don't worry about whether you are doing it right, just blow and draw on that hole and listen to the sound you get.

3. Now, narrow your lips as if you were going to whistle. Don't make a sound. You only need to position your lips so there is a small hole – enough space to play a single note.

4. Blow and draw again and listen. You should hear one note played clearly and cleanly. If you still hear more than one note, you haven't pursed your lips enough. Narrow them further and try again. You can stand before a mirror and watch what you are doing – this might make it easier.

A Good Tone

Put the harmonica in your lips, not on them, to get a better tone. This allows the lips to create a seal and play stronger notes. The trick is not to make your lips flat, or you won't get the seal. This will result in you needing to put more work in to get a decent tune out of the harmonica, which is tiring.

You should also have your jaw lowered, almost as if a hot potato were in your mouth. Raise your tongue a little at the back, but drop it at the front to expand your oral cavity. This might seem somewhat counter-intuitive, especially when your mouth shape has been restricted for a while, and you might even feel like you are going backward. However, this is a must if you want to learn how to play single notes. Practice really does make perfect in this case; eventually, you will get it. Your aim is to make this technique second nature when you play your harmonica to play powerful notes. Later, you'll see how to use this technique when actually playing, but for now, just practice the mouth position and get a single note.

Practice Exercises

When you reach the stage where you can produce one note on a hole, you must practice blowing and drawing single notes on every hole. The best exercise for this is the major scale, as below:

4 -4 5 -5 6 -6 7

Each number relates to a hole, so 4 means you should blow on hole 4, while -4 means drawing on it.

Try to play this left to right and then right to left. Listen as you play and, if you can, record any progress you make. Remember, maintain the same mouth shape to achieve clean notes when you move from one hole to the next.

Tongue Blocking

You must master the tongue-blocking method if you wish to advance your musical abilities. Continue reading to learn how to do it and why it will give your music a completely new dimension.

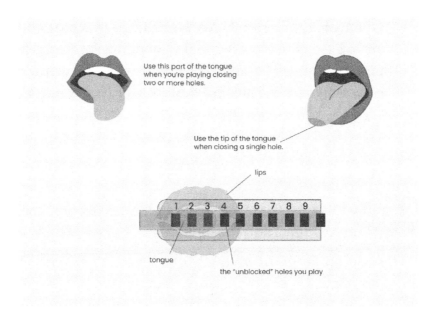

12. You must master the tongue-blocking method if you wish to advance your musical abilities. Source: https://lezionidiarmonica.it/assets/images/embouchure2-897x654.jpg

Why Tongue Blocking Works

Learning to tongue block has the following advantages:

- **Increased Volume**: Your notes will be significantly louder when you learn to tongue block than if you don't. When playing in a band, this enables you to fill the stage and stand out above the other instruments.

- **Clear Tone:** Because your tongue acts as a filter when you block, the sound is significantly richer and smoother. Particularly when you play multiple notes at once, this balances the tone.

- **Greater Ease for Note Bending:** By controlling airflow, tongue blocking makes bending simpler. This makes it much simpler to create vibrato, which is essential for musicians playing rock and blues music.

What You Need

- A harmonica
- The right posture

You must have a harmonica to learn how to tongue block. It doesn't matter which key it is.

The appropriate posture is also necessary. Whether you choose to stand or sit, make sure your harmonica is held correctly. Put your lips around it, being careful not to get your teeth on the reeds. Put the tip of your tongue right behind the blow note reeds as you extend it slightly.

Let your jaw drop. Take some time to unwind before you begin as if it's too tense, your tones won't be clear. To get it correct, practice your breathing now:

- To fill your lungs with air, inhale slowly and deeply. To exhale, use your diaphragm to push air out of your lungs while hissing.

To improve your ability to control your breathing, practice breathing from your diaphragm rather than your chest. You may get a steadier harmonica tone by breathing properly, so keep working on it until you master it.

How to Do a Basic Tongue Block

First, read these basic steps and then go through the more detailed explanation below.

Step One

Put your tongue close to the mouthpiece on the bottom of the plate, in between the reed plates.

Step Two

Press your tongue against the holes firmly to create a proper seal. This stops the air from going through the plate.

Step Three

Blow into your harmonica when you are confident your tongue is positioned correctly. You should play one note – the note not being blocked by the tongue.

Step Four

Lastly, slide your tongue along the reed plates, back and forth, leading to the note's pitch changing. This lets you play different notes.

Now, let's go into this in more detail.

Tongue Placement:

- Ensure that your tongue is loose and flat.

- The wider part of your tongue should cover multiple holes while you play the harmonica. Raise it so it rests on the roof of your mouth. Make sure your tongue is back far enough to ensure that all openings are shut.

Seal the Hole Off:

Only when your tongue restricts the airflow while you play can proper tongue blocking be accomplished. Cover the air holes with the tip of your tongue to accomplish this.

If your tongue is rounded, the sound is just distorted, thus, you should teach yourself to avoid doing this. Make sure your tongue is flat and firmly placed against the holes to get a crisp, clear sound. Additionally, to prevent air from escaping, make sure your lips form a tight seal.

Let's get back to our single notes.

Single Notes Part Two

Apart from tongue blocking, you need to learn a couple of other techniques to play single notes successfully.

- **Drawing and Blowing:** You should learn these two fundamental techniques: blowing and drawing. Blowing involves forcing air from your lungs into the harmonica's reed, while drawing involves pulling air out. You must become proficient in using your tongue, lips, and diaphragm for both.

- **Overblowing:** This method involves exhaling more air than usual in order to assist you in achieving high notes. The overblowing method enables you to produce a more expressive sound.

- **Bending:** Using your breath and manipulation of the shape of your tongue to control the reeds, while using this technique, you can lower the pitch of notes. Your voice becomes more soulful as a result.

Embouchure

The proper embouchure is essential for playing harmonica single notes. The word "mouth position" on a harmonica is technically referred to as "embouchure," and the Pucker is the one that is most frequently employed on the 10-hole diatonic harmonica. To do this, insert your upper lip at the top of the harmonica's mouthpiece with your lower lip curved over your bottom teeth.

Your tongue should not be touching the reeds but rather on the top portion of the mouthpiece. Regardless of the hole in which you play a single note, you should use this embouchure. You should modify your tongue position and airflow to achieve the desired sound. You should do this since it will help you manage your breath and tone.

Techniques

The table below shows you a few different techniques:

TECHNIQUE	DESCRIPTION
Blowing a single note	Blowing into the harmonica and playing a single note
Tongue blocking	Blocking different harmonica chambers with your tongue to play single notes
Split chords	Playing chords in a split manner using the lips and tongue to play many single notes
Octaves	Playing two single notes simultaneously; one should

	be one octave higher than the other
Bending	Manipulating a single note's pitch by changing breath control and air pressure
Overblowing	Increasing the air pressure to play a note one octave above the note that should be played
Vibrato	Changing the air pressure and your breath control to oscillate a single note's pitch

So, let's review. You need to hold the harmonica correctly when playing single notes. Your index fingers should be cupped around the instrument in a C-shape, and your thumbs should be on the back plate. When blowing into the harp, keep your lips open and use your tongue to guide the air through the proper hole. Make sure your tongue does not touch the reed, and keep your throat relaxed at the back to produce a clear sound. While playing your single note, inhale and exhale to create a vibrato.

See what tones and sounds you can generate by experimenting with the position of your tongue and your breathing.

Octaves

HOLE NUMBER	NOTE NAME	OCTAVE
1	C	4
2	D	4
3	E	4
4	F	4
5	G	4
6	A	4
7	B	4
8	C	5
9	D	5
10	E	5
11	F	5
12	G	5
13	A	5
14	B	5

A harmonica is typically built with three octaves of notes. The holes symbolize the notes, and each hole generates two distinct notes, depending on if you're drawing or blowing. Above are the notes for both octaves.

Harmonics

One of the most crucial methods for playing single notes is harmonics. You must understand how to create air pressure in order to know how to manufacture one. This occurs when the tongue is utilized to seal off an air leak. To do this, you briefly press your tongue against the roof of your mouth before releasing it. As a result, the air pressure rises, which causes the harp to vibrate.

Once you can do that, you must learn the three harmonic types you can produce:

- **Overblow:** This method involves exhaling more air than usual in order to assist you in achieving high notes. The overblowing method enables you to produce a more expressive sound.

- **Overdraw:** This requires you to inhale, drawing air from the reed. This creates air pressure, which leads to vibration in the reed.

- **Split:** This involves blocking the holes between notes in a chord, effectively splitting one chord into two harmony notes.

When you understand these, you can play the single notes. You must find the right pitch of the note and then use the right hole to get that note.

Vibrato

To create vibrato:

1. Use your diaphragm to bend the note slightly.

2. Repeat and release quickly.

3. Ensure that the vibrato is consistent and steady.

4. Vary the intensity and speed to get different sounds.

Practice Exercises

NOTES	EXERCISE	REPETITIONS
C	Blow a single C	10
D	Blow a single D	10
E	Blow a single E	10
F	Blow a single F	10
G	Blow a single G	10
A	Blow a single A	10
B	Blow a single B	10

Do these exercises in order and succession, beginning with C and ending with B. When you have played everything, repeat several more times. The more you practice, the better you will get at single notes.

Embouchures

The two most common embouchures are pucker and tongue block, both of which were discussed earlier. Now, we will recap them and give you some detailed information.

Pucker

As you learned earlier, this is one of the easiest embouchures to learn, and you should learn and master this one before you move on to tongue bending. Here are some tips to help you:

- Open your mouth with your lips relaxed.

- Place the harmonica between your lips, ensuring the front touches your lips at the left and right corners.

- Cushion your lips against the instrument to stop it from sliding.

- Use your lips to breathe in and out gently.

- When you are playing your harmonica, allow it to slip forward a little, creating a small opening, like a pout. At no time must the corners of your lips stop touching the harmonica.

- In this position, you can isolate one note by shifting your lips forward more than you normally would. Keep your lips gentle and move consistently.

- Focus on the air while it leaves your mouth; you will likely hear a hissing sound – most beginners do! You can fix this by ensuring the harmonica still touches the corners of your lips and keeping the air in your mouth directed towards the instrument.

- To align the gap with your mouth, simply move the harmonica a tiny bit. If you find it difficult to play single notes, move the slideways of the harmonica just as you pout your lips outward.

- Your single notes will sound better if you place the harmonica firmly inside your mouth. Avoid pressing on it.

- Achieving an airtight, relaxed seal that produces a tone requires patience. It takes time to learn, and only practice will get you there.

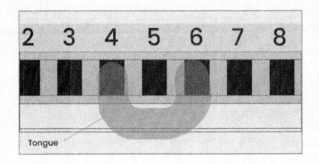

13. *The proper embouchure is essential for playing harmonica single notes. The pucker position.*

Tongue Block

Again, as you learned earlier, this technique is great for playing notes with special effects. For example, it can help you produce a full, rich tone. Yes, you can accomplish this by using the puckering technique, but tongue blocking is far more natural and feels better.

The following is a recap of what was covered earlier, just to ensure it is firmly in your mind:

- Relax your lips and fully open your mouth.

- The front of the harp should brush your lips at the left and right corners as you place it between your lips.

- Use your lips to cushion the harp so that it won't slide unless you want it to.

- Breathe slowly in and out using your lips.

- To make a space between the right corner of your lips and the matching edge of your tongue, press the tip of your tongue down towards your lower lip.

- Raise the top of your tongue so that it pushes against the harmonica.

- Keep your focus on the air as it escapes, and move your harmonica left or right. This should result in a single note. Ensure the mouth opening is small, allowing you to produce that single note. At the same time, your airflow must be right to strengthen your note.

Moving between Notes

If you can produce a single note, be proud of yourself. It isn't the easiest thing to learn, but your practice and consistency will pay off. However, now comes the hammer blow. You will never find a melody that consists of only one note. That means you must learn how to move from one note to another to play a melody.

When it comes to moving between notes when playing the harmonica, there are a few rules you must learn:

- Change the course of your breath from blow to draw and draw to blow. When you do this, only your breathing must change.

- You can change holes by sliding the harp on the right or left of your mouth as well as using your tongue to determine which hole is being utilized.

- You must know which note you want. Every hole produces different notes.

- Ensure your breath direction and holes are synchronized.

Advanced Techniques

While this is meant to be a beginner's book, I want to go over a couple of advanced tongue-blocking techniques you can try on your harmonica.

Creating Chord Textures

Your tongue can assist you in adding texture when you play chords, similar to how a guitarist might strum a complex pattern rather than merely playing the chord's notes once. You can use the hammer, split, and shimmer chord textures, among others.

Producing the Chord Rake

A chord rake is produced when you rake your tongue over the harmonica holes, right to left or left to right. Some notes will always be audible, while the rest will be blocked by your tongue. Raking your tongue over this combination causes it to constantly alter, giving it a texture akin to an up-and-down guitar strum.

This is how you do it:

1. Perform a chord with at least three holes.

2. Place your tongue on one side of the harmonica, making sure that some of it is covered and some is uncovered.

3. Move your tongue up and down the harmonica while playing the chord.

By making sure that the edge of your tongue hits each corner of your mouth, make sure you cover the entire length of the harp, as far right and left as you can. You can also achieve the best results by doing this.

Playing a Chord Hammer

A chord hammer can be added to a melody note. This is a series of chords repeated in quick succession, played while the melody note is sounding. Although it sounds like an impressive skill, playing it is really quite simple.

1. Cover enough holes on the harmonica with your tongue so that only one note is playing.

2. Rapidly remove your tongue from the harp and replace it just as rapidly.

3. If you alternate between having your tongue in the on and off positions, you will hear an undulating sound that sounds almost as if you are using your tongue as a hammer to strike a series of quick blows.

You don't need to move very quickly because the effect will make it appear as though you are moving twice as fast. If you move too quickly, you risk losing control.

A hammered split is similar, but you begin with a split. This is where your tongue is positioned on the harmonica, you should have an open hole on either side. The movements are exactly the same as the hammer, lifting and replacing your tongue quickly.

The Shimmer

Shimmers are comparable to chord rakes, except instead of playing all the notes in your mouth, you alternate between the left and right side notes. Two methods can result in a shimmer:

- Move the tip of your tongue tip as if it were a chord rake.

- Maintain the position of the tip of your tongue.

When you do this, the tip of your tongue begins to rock backward in a wagging manner. It covers the left and right holes alternately as it rocks from left to right.

This causes the tip of your tongue to rock in place because you start the wagging motion from further back on your tongue. It alternately covers the holes on the left and right as it bounces side to side.

To eliminate chord tones that don't go with those a guitarist or pianist is playing, employ a shimmer. Compared to a chord hammer or rake, it also delivers a more subdued effect.

The Tongue Slap

Tongue blocking offers plenty of different techniques to try, and one of the most common is tongue slap. This is best described as a short chord immediately followed by the highest available note played as a single note using the tongue-blocking embouchure described earlier.

Here's how to do a tongue slap:

1. Position your mouth over the 2nd, 3rd, and 4th holes – the first hole can also be included if you want.

2. Position your tongue over the 1st, 2nd, and 3rd holes. This tongue-blocking embouchure allows you to play the 4th hole. To check you are in the right position, breathe in and out; you should only be able to hear the 4th hole.

3. Lift your tongue from the harmonica without breathing.

4. Breathe in to start an inhale chord.

5. Place your tongue quickly over the 1st, 2nd, and 3rd holes to block them; again, only hole 4 should be playing.

Moving between the 4th and 5th steps should be very quick. You should not be able to hear a chord and a single note, only a single note with a heavy push before it. This sounds even better when you master it and play it amplified.

When to Use

This technique works great when playing simple riffs, making them sound more interesting and bigger than they are. Don't overdo it. Mix a few unslapped notes in, too.

Corner Switching

If you play a single note on your harmonica, but the next note is a few holes away, it can be quite difficult to get to it. The biggest challenge lies in hitting the right hole when you move, and there is a high chance you'll hit the notes in between by accident. That's where corner switching comes in.

Corner switching lets you move quickly from a note on the right to one on the left, and all you need to do is move your tongue from right to left or vice versa.

Here's how to do it:

- Position your mouth in the middle of the harmonica, ensuring that the right and left corners of your mouth are in front of the 1st and 2nd notes of the leap.

- Ensure that your tongue is on the harmonica and the hole relating to the first note is open. Block the rest.

- Open the first hole and position your tongue on the second.

- This is somewhat similar to the shimmer, and you can improve on it even more when you use the following tips:

- Start with hole 4 and draw on the right of your tongue.

- Inhale and position your tongue on the right, blocking hole 4 and releasing hole 1.

- Go back to the left, covering hole 4 draw.

- Remain there and play until you reach hole 6 blow.

- Play it and take your tongue to the right, blocking hole 6 and releasing hole 3.

- Return to hole 6, blow, and play the remaining notes.

It should look like this:

4 1 4 4 5 6 3 6 6 5

Practice this frequently, but start slowly. You can increase your speed as you get the hang of it.

Tongue Blocking DOs and DON'Ts

To finish this chapter, here are a series of DOs and DON'TS you should follow when you learn to tongue block.

1. DON'T Skip the Basics

While tongue blocking provides you with plenty of new textures to play about with, such as octaves, slaps, and more, you must learn to play single notes perfectly first. Trying a new technique is always tempting, but you must believe me when I say it won't work. Be patient, start at the beginning, and work your way up.

2. DO Re-Learn Simple Songs You Can Already Play with the Pucker Embouchure

If you can play a simple melody using the pucker embouchure, you should re-learn it with the tongue block. That way, you won't need to worry about how the melody should sound or whether you've played the tabs correctly. This leaves you free to focus on the tongue-blocking technique and getting your mouth shape right to play consistently clear, clean notes. Where possible, record yourself practicing. Listen to the recording and identify where you need to improve.

3. DON'T Force the Air

Regardless of mouth shape, this point is important. You might find yourself trying to force the air out when you tongue block. This could be because your mouth shape is larger, or it could be the tongue position. Regardless of the reason, there is a tendency to push the air out too much. If you do, your harmonica will not sound very nice, or you'll struggle to play it. That leads to your blowing more, and the sound will be even worse. This is a habit you need to break. You must learn to relax and teach yourself natural breathing, and you'll find tongue blocking much easier to master.

4. DO Experiment with How You Hold Your Head

As you watch harmonica players, you might notice that some press their harp against their cheek. This ensures a tight seal, which leads to better airflow. You notice this more when the harmonica is being played amplified, as it's important to ensure that the air gets to the microphone. Try it yourself and see how much difference it makes to your comfort and sound. All players are different. What works for one may not work for another.

5. DON'T Press Your Tongue on the Harmonica Too Hard

The tongue block technique requires you to position your tongue on the harmonica to block certain notes. Press too hard, and it's nothing more than a waste of your energy. It also causes your muscles to tense, and it could negatively affect your sound. Learn to be mindful. Be aware of what you are doing all the time, learn to relax, and allow your tongue to sit gently but precisely on the harmonica. This will result in cleaner, fuller notes without you having to expend so much energy.

6. DO Practice Playing All the Notes

You must get to grips with playing every hole your harmonica has. Depending on your position on the instrument, there are some things to consider. For example, basic tongue blocking requires your mouth shape to be four harmonic holes wide, using your tongue to block the three lower holes. This means you can play the top hole out of the four. However, what if a four-hole width isn't achievable? Some players will make their mouth shape smaller, reducing it to a three-hole, then two, while others change the shape to play lower notes while blocking high ones. Some will use the pucker technique on the lower holes. It really is up to you. Do whatever is comfortable, but you must consider all your options if you are to play every available note.

7. DON'T Soak Your Instrument

Even if the world's top players do this, you shouldn't. It's one of the old techniques used on harmonicas with wooden combs and is said to make them airtight. This might work for a short while, but when it dries, the wood will swell, and that could cause cracking. At best, it just won't be comfortable to play, no matter what embouchure you choose to use. It's even worse for those who use tongue blocking because splintered wood and the soft tissue of your tongue don't go well together!

8. DO Listen to Legends

Find and listen to legends like William Clarke, Big Walter, and Little Walter, all known for their mastery of tongue blocking. When you listen carefully, you can get inside the heads of the best players ever to master this technique, and you might even get some new ideas to try.

9. DON'T Feel like You Need to Tongue Block Every Note

While practicing tongue blocking on all notes is great, don't let it get you down if you can't make it work on everything. Use a combination of tongue blocking and puckering; plenty of players do it, and you can produce some great sounds if you get it right.

10. DO enjoy yourself

Tongue blocking is not easy to learn, especially if you are more proficient with puckering. But don't get miserable if it takes you a while to learn. This is a great journey, and you need to enjoy it. Relax, take your time, and have fun.

11. DON'T Expect Miracles

Tongue blocking on your harmonica is nothing more than a foundation. Mastering it isn't going to make you the world's number-one player overnight! You still need to learn and practice timing, listening, repertoire, and much more besides. That can take years, not days. Learn to accept this and, once again, enjoy the journey.

Chapter 5: Learning to Play Simple Melodies

Before moving on to slightly more advanced topics, let's take some time to play a few simple melodies. We'll start with a brief look at reading music, then we'll play a few melodies before looking at techniques to change breath and hole and some listening skills.

14. *In order to master the harmonica, you must learn how to read its music first. Source: https://unsplash.com/photos/k4WJjF0-3Y0*

Reading Harmonica Music

It's crucial to comprehend harmonica tablature since it specifies which hole to play and whether to draw or blow to achieve a particular note. In some tablatures, arrows are used to denote blows and draws, respectively. The hole you need to blow into is indicated by a plus (+) sign, whilst the hole you need to draw from is shown by a negative (-).

Sometimes, an apostrophe is used, for example 2'. This indicates a half-step bend on the given hole.

Here's an example:

- -2' – this tells you to draw bend down half a step at hole 2.

- -2" – this tells you to draw bend down a whole step at hole 2.

- -2''' – this tells you to draw bend down one and a half steps at hole 2.

- You can apply the same to the blow bends:

- +9' – this tells you to blow bend down half a step at hole 9.

- +9" – this tells you to blow bend down a whole step at hole 9.

Let's Play Music

Let's take a break and see how much you have learned. Try playing the following on your harmonica:

+4-4 +5-5 +6-6 -7+7

Now let's add to this. Use the above scale to play the following:

+4 -4 +5-5 +6-6 -7+7

You should have spotted that you played a very famous notation:

Do Re Mi Fa So La Ti Do

Let's try the following songs in any order you want.

Mary Had a Little Lamb

Everyone knows this classic kid's song, and it's a great one for beginners to start on. It uses just 3 holes, so you can play a melody without needing to move around too much:

5 -4 4 -4 5 5 5

Mary had a little lamb

-4 -4 -4

Little lamb

5 6 6

Little lamb

5 -4 4 -4 5 5 5

Mary had a little lamb

5 -4 -4 5 -4 4

Whose fleece was white as snow

Edelweiss

If you've watched "The Sound of Music," you'll know this song about a little flower found in the Alps. It's a song of love and hope and will stretch your learning because you must play up to the 8th hole.

5 6 -8 7 6 -5

Edelweiss, edelweiss

5 5 5 -5 6 -6 6

Every morning you greet me

5 6 -8

Small and white

7 6 -5

Clean and bright

5 6 6 -6 -7 7 7

You look happy to meet me

-8 6 6 -7 -6 6 5 6 7

Blossom of snow, may you bloom and grow

-6 7 -8 7 -7 6

Bloom and grow for-ev-er

5 6 -8 7 6 -5

Edelweiss, edelweiss

5 6 6 -6 -7 7 7

Bless my homeland for-ev-er

This Old Man

Another classic kid's song, this one has an unforgettable rhythm. It's one of the best songs for teaching beginners how to quickly shift from one note to another.

6 5 6 6 5 6

This old man, he played ONE

-6 6 -5 5 -4 5 -5

He played knick-knack on my THUMB

5 -5 6 4 4 4 4

With a knick-knack, paddywhack

4 -4 5 -5 6

Give a dog a bone

6 -4 -4 -5 5 -4 4

This old man came rolling home

Humpty Dumpty

Everyone knows this nursery thyme, and the last line lets you practice jumping between notes that aren't next to one another.

5 6 -5 -6 6 -6 -7 7

Humpty Dumpty sat on a wall

5 6 -5 -6 6 6 5 4 -4

Humpty Dumpty had a great fall

5 5 6 -5 -5 -6 6 -6 -7 7

All the king's horses and all the king's men

8 8 7 -9 -9 8 -8 7 -7 7

Couldn't put Humpty together again

Sound of Silence

This is a famous hit from 1964 for Simon & Garfunkel, and it works really well for the harmonica:

-4 -4 -5 -5 -6 -6 6

Hello darkness, my old friend

4 4 4 5 5 6 6 -5

I've come to talk with you again

-5 -5 -5 -6 -6 7 7 -8 -8 7

Because a vision softly creeping

-5 -5 -6 -6 7 7 -8 -8 7

Left its seeds while I was sleeping

-5 -5 -8 -8 -8 8 -9 -9 8 -8 7

And the vision that was planted in my brain

-8 7 -6

Still remains

-5 -5 -5 7 5 -5 -4

Within the sound of silence

Row Row Row Your Boat

Yet another kid's song that works really well for the harmonica and allows you to practice playing a four-hole range.

4 4 4 -4 5

Row, row, row your boat

5 -4 5 -5 6

Gently down the stream

7 7 7 6 6 6 5 5 5 4 4 4

Me-rr-ily, me-rr-ily, me-rr-ily, me-rr-ily

6 -5 5 -4 4

Life is but a dream

Happy Birthday to You

We've all sung this one at one time or another, even if it was just during the pandemic while washing our hands! This song requires you to go up to hole 9.

6 6 -6 6 7 -7

Happy birthday to you

6 6 -6 6 -8 7

Happy birthday to you

6 6 9 8 7 -7 -6

Happy birthday dear [someone]

-9 -9 8 7 -8 7

Happy birthday to you

On Top of Old Smokey

A popular folk song in the Southern USA, this is often played around campfires and is a good one to learn.

4 4 5 6 7 -6

On top of old Smokey

-6 -5 6 -6 6

All covered with snow

4 4 5 6 6 -4

I lost my true lover

5 -5 -5 5 -4 4

From (a-)courting too slow

Home on the Range

Another popular song in the USA, this cowboy song needs you to go up as far as hole 9 to get to the upper register.

6 6 7 -8 8

Oh give me a home

7 -7 -6 -9 -9 -9

Where the buffalo roam

8 -9 9 7 7 7 -7 7 -8

And the deer and the antelope play

6 6 7 -8 8

Where seldom is heard

7 -7 -6 -9 -9 -9

A discouraging word

-9 -9 8 -8 7 -7 7 -8 7

And the skies are not cloudy all day

9 -9 8 -8 8

Home, home on the range

6 6 7 7 7 7 -7 7 -8

Where the deer and the antelope play

6 6 7 -8 8

Where seldom is heard

7 -7 -6 -9 -9 -9

A discouraging word

-9 -9 8 -8 7 -7 7 -8 7

And the skies are not cloudy all day

Ode to Joy

The last song is a classical piece that will challenge you, especially as a beginner, as it is more difficult than the previous songs.

5 5 -5 6 6 -5 5 -4 4 4 -4 5 5 -4 -4

5 5 -5 6 6 -5 5 -4 4 4 -4 5 -4 4 4

-4 -4 5 4 -4 5 -5 5 4 -4 5 -5 5 -4 4 -4 3 5

5 5 -5 6 6 -5 5 -4 4 4 -4 5 -4 4 4

Exploring Breath and Hole Changes

Learning to change your breath and holes is very important to your harmonica journey. We'll start with breath changes, followed by hole changes, and then we'll look at alternating them and doing them simultaneously.

Breath Changes

We'll start with breath changes when playing single notes:

1. Play blow hole 4, ensuring your note is single, isolated, and clean.

2. Play it, and then play draw 4 by inhaling.

3. When you inhale, you should not hear any other notes, if you do, you might be doing one of the following:

- Changing your mouth opening shape. Practice keeping your lips still when you change from blow to draw and back again.

- Moving the harmonica in your mouth. It only needs to slide left or right slightly, and you'll play more than one note. Practice keeping the harmonica still when you switch between blow and draw.

4. Switch between blowing and drawing hole 4, aiming to play clean single notes as you start each new breath.

When you can achieve this in hole 4, try it with other holes on your harmonica.

Hole Changes

It might sound easy to move between the holes on your harmonica, but you must know how far you have to move. Over time, as you gain experience, your muscle memory will be your guide, but as a beginner, you must learn to move and listen to what happens. Try this to get started:

1. Play hole 4 blow and sustain it.

2. Exhale, sliding your hands using your forearms, and move the harmonica left until you hear the hole 5 note.

- If blow 4 and 5 sound together, move the instrument left a bit more until you can only hear 5.

- You'll likely hear blows 5 and 6 or only 6 if you go too far. In this case, move the harmonica right a little until you can only hear blow 5.

    3. If you have to take a breath, drop your lower jaw a little, ensuring the harmonica rests on your lower lip, then take a breath and raise your jaw again to continue playing.

    4. When you hear blow 5 played clearly, move the instrument right, and play blow 4.

    5. Alternate between the two a few times, ensuring you always get a clear single note each time.

When you move to the next hole, listen; you want to hear the sound of the transition between the two notes. Your aim should be to hear the first note and then the second, not both together, but this will take practice.

As you move left to get to the higher holes, you might feel like the harmonica was attached to hole 4 by a piece of elastic. You can overcome this:

    1. Play a clear single note, and immediately slide the harmonica left and right, taking it from holes 4 to 10 and then back again and do it quickly.

    2. Forget about the holes being played; just practice allowing the harmonica to slide easily left and right.

Alternating Breath to Hole Changes

Once you have mastered smooth hole changes, practice stopping at every hole and adding a breath change. Alternate between blow and draw on each hole, then move to the next one.

Note the breath mark at the end of each second measure; you might need to take a breath.

When you move to the next hole, try to play the two notes with one breath so you can hear where you are going.

Simultaneous Hole and Breath Changes

Listen to yourself as you change the direction of your breath when moving between holes. As you make the move, you should not hear an audible switch. However, if you make the change in one single breath without changing direction, your muscle memory will tell you where you need to go.

When playing scales in the middle register, you play a draw on the left and move to a blow note on the right:

1. First, change holes without changing breath.

2. Then, change holes at the same time as changing breath.

3. Extend this through the harmonica's entire middle register.

You might also do the opposite - play a blow note on the left and move to a draw on the right. This happens in some melodies, particularly those played in holes 1 to 6, but you do this on holes 7 to 10 for the scale.

Improving Your Listening Skills

Ask yourself a question: why are you learning to play the harmonica? Is it for fun? Or have you listened to professionals playing the instrument and felt something deep inside you? Something that tells you this is meant to be your vocation in life.

By its very nature, the harmonica is considered expressive, and you can use literally hundreds of techniques. You can create shrill, warm, bright, tense, happy, melancholy, or jubilant sounds, and tons more in between.

However, before you can even consider any of those techniques to create your unique sound, you need to learn to listen. You have to hear those techniques in action, how they work together, where they work, and, importantly, where they don't. You must also understand how they can be incorporated into your own playing style.

This part of the chapter is dedicated to your listening skills and their importance in developing your sound. When you understand what pro players do, you can try to emulate their style to start with and then develop it into your own.

What Makes Your Sound Unique?

Most people consider sound as coming from the equipment they use – this is common among beginners.

While the equipment certainly has its role, it isn't as important as you might have thought. Sure, the combination of equipment you use – harmonica, mics, and amps – does contribute, but if the initial sound is rubbish, you can't make good when you amplify it. You need to get a great sound acoustically before trying to amplify it.

So, what's the most important ingredient?

It's all about your style. It's about how you present the notes, about your embouchure, rhythm, phrasing, and structure. This works well for acoustic and amplified playing.

Focused vs. Unfocused Development

You should continuously listen to your favorite players as you develop your skills and style. When you do this, you internalize their style, albeit subconsciously. Some of it will appear in your style and sound, and this is known as unfocused development. While nothing is wrong with this, it has one downside – you do not control what goes into your sound, and you have no idea if it is technically right.

15. You should practice and choose your sound carefully. Source: https://pixabay.com/photos/nursery-toddler-child-uk-baby-718788/

You need to start with ear training to move from this to focused development.

Ear training is one of the best tools at your disposal to improve your listening skills, enabling you to tell the difference between what you hear and helping you break down how those sounds are produced.

When you do this, you get an active choice in what you include in your style, and you can learn to tweak certain techniques to suit you.

First, you need to train yourself to hear the nuances and sounds before understanding how they are produced. Then, you can try to reproduce them and compare your efforts to the original. It's quite simple; if you can't hear it, you can't play it.

So, what do you need to listen for?

A few building blocks were mentioned earlier – embouchure, rhythm, phrasing, etc. – and these provide the player's sound. To go deep with your ear training and active listening, it's imperative that you listen to your favorite player a lot and note down what you hear. The more you listen actively, the more you will hear.

One way of doing this is using a worksheet to take your notes. On it, list all the techniques the player uses. Then, note how often that technique is used – always, sometimes, or never. While doing this, listen for nuances that you can note down, too.

Here's an idea of how your worksheet could look – it's very simple:

Artist Worksheet

Artist:

Technique	Always	Sometimes	Never	Notes

To get you up and running, think about the following techniques. As you get better, your ears will hear more, and you'll spot more nuances and maybe some different techniques.

- **Embouchure:** Most pro players use tongue blocking for most of their music. Try to spot if the player changes to puckering and note when they do it. If they tend to use puckering the most, try to figure out how they incorporate the chords.

Presentation of the Notes:

- **Clean Notes:** These are single notes with no air played into any holes on either side. This creates a clean monophonic sound. By contrast, a dirty note is the main note, with a little of the notes on either side played at the same time. You must learn to understand the difference between these and the feeling each gives to the music.

- **Chords:** A set of three or more notes played simultaneously. Do remember one thing: the line between a chord played on the 2nd, 3rd, and 4th holes and a dirty note with hole 3 as the main one played with a little of holes 2 and 4 is very fine. Learn to tell the difference.

- **Octave Splits:** These are two notes played together but three holes apart. For example, playing holes 6 and 9. If the harmonica is well-tuned, you may struggle to hear an octave split and not one hole being played much stronger.

- **Fake Splits:** These splits are not true octaves. i.e., if you play holes 2 and 5 at the same time, it is a minor 7th.

Musical Effects:

- **Flutter:** In this technique, the flutter is used to allow some of the chords to sound beneath the note the player is playing

- **Tongue Slap:** In this technique, the player plays the full chord for a very short time, then uses their tongue to shut it off, so the only note being played is the melody note.

- **Pull Slap:** Much like the tongue slap, the notes are blocked first, and then the player performs a sharp tongue slap.

- **Articulations:** The player begins these chords or notes with an articulated syllable, such as "yah," "ka," "do," or "ha."

- **Tremolo:** This gives your sound a fluttering or trembling effect, and you can do it with your hand or throat.

- **Vibrato:** This uses pulses from the hand, throat, or gut to alter the pitch.

- **Phrasing:** This is when you put notes into groups to make the music sound more interesting, and it can be done in several ways. Typically, it is instinctive, which is why some people's music sounds so expressive. When you listen to your favorite players, make notes of the long and short phrases and all that comes between them. Note the beat a phrase starts on. Does it always start on the first beat, or does it differ?

- **Rhythm:** Note if the musical piece has a steady or unsteady rhythm. Do the notes get played on the beat, or do they dance around it? Are they swinging? Does the musician use chords in creating their rhythm?

- **Tension:** This has an important role in your music, as does release. Musicians use several techniques to do this, but one of the more advanced ways is to pick out single notes to create tension. The more chords you listen to, the more adept you will become at doing this.

- **Chord Tones:** These notes are used with the chords to create tension. Listen to how they are used in the music and note them down.

- **Scale Tones:** These notes are found in certain scales and are all related to the tonic. Note how the musician uses them for resolution and tension.

- **Blue Notes:** These are not played at the standard pitch. Usually, they are a quartertone or semitone off, giving them their distinctive feel.

- **Repetition and Structure:** These phrases are sequenced to develop musical passages. Listen for repeated structures.

- **Solos and Fills vs. Backup Playing**: Listen to see if the harmonica is being played throughout the vocals. Is the musician using fills? These are riffs played between each vocal phrase.

Developing Your Harmonica Sound

This subject will be discussed in greater depth later in the book, but here's an idea of how to develop your sound for now.

You first need to understand what you like. Do you like fast tongue-slap phrases? Long phrases? Or something completely different? You can only start developing a technique when you know what you want to achieve, and then you can bring it into your harmonica playing.

Here's how to do this:

1. Understand how to perform a technique by breaking it down into individual components.

2. Have an idea in your head of how you think the technique should sound.

3. Play it and compare it to how you thought it should sound. Repeat it consistently, and you will eventually perform it better.

4. When you have learned that technique, put some context to it by using it in a phrase or song. Then, you can experiment with using it.

You would need to follow these steps for every technique you want to include. Start with one, learn it well, and then add another. Eventually, you will have several techniques in your repertoire. When you first learn a technique, overuse it to the extent that you get fed up with it! That way, it will become second nature.

Sharper Listening Skills

It's really quite simple. You need to have excellent listening skills to understand what your favorite players do and to be able to replicate it. The above steps will help you understand the sounds produced by different techniques.

Ear training is one of the most valuable skills, especially hearing and recognizing intervals. It helps you understand how the harmonica is laid out and how it works, not to mention the sounds different combinations of holes will produce. It will also help you learn to recognize what a root note sounds like and how to tell if a note is above or below it.

Chapter 6: Learning to Play Chords

Chords and chord progressions are integral to learning to play music on a harmonica. All music includes them, and, as a new player, learning about chords will help you understand the relationship between notes and chord sequences. They can also help you better understand written music.

The simplest chord is a triad, and it contains three notes.

- You start from the root of the triad. For example, you build a C triad from the C note, a D triad from the D note, and so on.

- The third of the triad. This is the note third up from the root. For example, if working with a C triad, the third is E.

- The fifth of the triad. Likewise, this is the fifth up. However, it is also the third up from the third. For example, a C triad's fifth is G.

A chain of thirds may also be a triad, for example:

C-E-G, E-G-B, G-B-D, B-D-F, D-F-A, F-A-C, A-C-E

Examine the note layout on a C harmonica; you will find a few of these.

- All the blow notes are a C triad – C, E, G.

- Each draw note has three triads:

- **G Triad:** G-B-D – first, second, third, and fourth holes

- **B Triad:** B-D-F – third, fourth, and fifth and seventh, eighth, and ninth holes

- **D Triad:** D-F-A – fourth, fifth, and sixth, and eighth, ninth, and tenth holes

Chords can be built on any scale degree by using the scale's notes. Chords are numbered using Roman numerals, depending on the scale degree you use in building the chord. For example, the C scale's first degree is C. The C chord becomes I, the D becomes II, and so on through the Roman numerals.

Basic Chord Types

There are four triad types, and each one has its own interval qualities:

- **Major Triad:** This comprises a major third and a perfect fifth. There are two majors on a C harmonica:

- **C Major:** Uses any blow notes on the harmonica

- **G Major:** Uses draw notes 1 through 4

- **Minor Triad:** This comprises a minor third and a perfect fifth. There is one minor triad on a C harmonica. It is the D minor triad and it can be found in two places:

- Draw holes 4, 5, and 6

- Draw holes 8, 9, and 10

- **Diminished Triad:** This comprises a minor third and a diminished fifth. There is one diminished triad on the C harmonica. It is the B diminished triad, and it is found in two places:

- Draw holes 3, 4, and 5

- Draw holes 7, 8, and 9

- **Augmented Triad:** This comprises a major third and an augmented fifth. There are no augmented triads built into a C harmonica.

- An augmented triad has a major third and an augmented fifth. Your C-harmonica doesn't have any built-in augmented triads.

Adding Notes

Provided it produces a good sound, any note can be added to a basic triad. For example, you would get a major 6th chord if you added the 6th to a major triad.

One of the most commonly used methods to extend a chord is to count odd scale degrees and add thirds. For example, with a basic triad of 1, 3, and 5, you could add 7, 9, 11, and so on to your chord.

However, it is worth noting that 9, 11, and 13 are known as compound intervals, which means they are larger than an octave:

- **9th degree:** the 2nd degree played one octave higher

- **11th degree:** the 4th degree played one octave higher

- **13th degree:** the 6th degree played one octave higher

You can help make your method clearer by numbering them in ascending order.

If you use a diatonic C harmonica, there are already some extended chords built-in:

- **G Major Chord:** The second, third, and fourth draw holes. Adding the fifth draw hole can extend this to a 7th chord. To extend it to a 9th, add the sixth draw hole.

- **B Diminished:** Has an added 7th - the third, fourth, fifth, and sixth draw holes.

- **D Minor:** With 6th chord – the fourth, fifth, sixth, and seventh draw holes

Chord Progressions

Most of the time, accompanying chords are played on other instruments, sometimes several that play the notes needed to make a chord. Some songs use one chord, but the majority have a sequence known as a chord progression. Each chord is played for a specific number of bars or beats in a progression.

16. Most of the time, accompanying chords are played on other instruments, sometimes several that play the notes needed to make a chord. Source: https://pixabay.com/photos/music-instruments-cymbals-2148627/

If you look at sheet music, the chord names are written above the melody. However, most of the time, a musician will use chord relationships to describe the progression. This is done using the Roman numeral I for the tonic-built chord. The scale degrees are then numbered, and a Roman numeral is used to name chords built on specific degrees.

Using relationships to name the chords allows you to switch easily between keys, which is far easier than having to translate letter names to keys. Once you learn what each of these translates to in a given key, you can simply input the new values when you change keys.

Some chords are more important than others. Those are the I, IV, and V chords, regardless of key. If you have ever heard anyone talking about simple tunes as something like an

I-IV-V progression, they usually refer to the chords in use, but be aware that chords can be in any sequence, not just that one.

Positioning Your Mouth

Playing chords typically requires the same mouth and hand positioning as tongue-blocking. However, in this case, your tongue should be positioned away from the holes at the bottom of the mouth. Because your lips and mouth naturally cover holes 3 and 4, the harmonica must be moved to ensure the right holes are covered. For example, playing a C major chord is done like this:

1. Position the harmonica in your mouth.

2. Move it so that the first, second, and third holes are aligned where your lips cover.

3. Blow notes 1, 2, and 3 by breathing out from your diaphragm. This produces the C major chord sound.

You will struggle to tell if you are playing the right chord notes until you are familiar with how the major, minor, and seventh chords sound. Begin by following the steps above to learn the C major chord. It should have a happy, bright sound. Once you know how that sounds, try the D minor chord by playing draw notes 4, 5, and 6 or 8, 9, and 10. It should sound the total opposite of the C major – brooding and dark rather than happy and bright. If the chords you want to play meet those two descriptions, there's a good chance you are playing the right notes.

When to Play Chords

The diatonic harmonica is limited in the number of chords it can produce. As such, you will probably never use it to play accompanying chords. Instead, you will probably use it in solos. For example, if you play guitar, you might play a chord progression on the guitar and a harmonic chord solo over the top – this is advanced stuff, though.

Playing Arpeggios

Because a limited number of chords are playable on diatonic harmonicas, some players will play arpeggios instead. These are a type of chord where each note is played on its own and not all at the same time. These tend to be used when chords can't be played on a specific harmonica.

For example, if your music called for an E minor, you would need to play an arpeggio with the same notes as the E minor chord, i.e., E, G, and B. Playing arpeggios requires that you know which notes the chord comprises and how to play them on your instrument.

Scales

It's useful to learn how to play scales on your harmonica. A scale consists of two notes that are one octave apart, with some of the pitches between them. There are many keys one could potentially play in and combine with other keys, which makes the possibilities endless. That said, most players use just a few standard scale types.

The notes in any given scale can be described in one of these three ways:

1. Name the notes belonging to the scale. The following two methods will usually determine those names.

2. Describe each step size in ascending order from one degree to the next in the scale, beginning at the tonic. Most of these steps will be S (semitones) or T (whole tone.) Each scale type is usually a pattern of semitones and tones to describe the steps as they ascend. For example, a major scale's step pattern is TTS TTTS.

3. Each scale step forms an interval with the tonic.

Chromatic and Diatonic Scales

There are two types of scales: chromatic and diatonic.

- **Chromatic scales** comprise all the notes of an octave, which is 12. If you include the note completing the octave, it becomes 13. The chromatic scale is not considered in any single key, instead, it is like an inventory of all the notes. A chromatic scale has a step pattern of SSSSSSSSSSSS.

- **Diatonic scales** comprise the seven notes of one key, for example, a piano's white keys.

Minor and Major Scales

The C harmonica scales are grouped into major, minor, and weird. The latter group is only weird until you learn and understand them. The minor and major scales have their own characteristics:

Major scales have the following characteristics:

- A major 3rd degree.

- If it is a standard major, its step pattern is TTS TTTS.

However, if it doesn't have the exact true major scale step pattern but still has a major 3rd degree, it is still considered a major scale.

Major scales built into the C harmonica are:

- **C:** All C major scale notes are included in the C harmonica.

- **F:** Creating a major scale requires that the B natural note is lowered a semitone to B♭ó.

- **A:** Creating a major scale requires raising the F natural note one semitone.

The most popular key for C harmonicas is not C, as you might think, but is G.

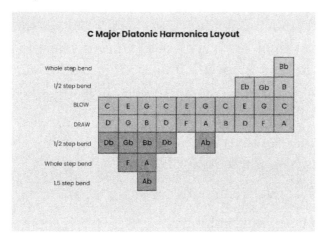

17. *The C major diatonic harmonica layout. Source: Minor scales have these characteristics: https://www.harmonica.com/wp-content/uploads/2021/01/C.png*

- A minor 3rd degree.
- The 6th and 7th degrees can be minor or major.

- A scale will be called a natural minor scale when the 6th and 7th scale degrees are raised one half-step or semitone.

Minor scales built into the C harmonica are:

- **A:** The natural minor scale
- **D:** Comprises B, which is a major 6th, giving melodies a haunting sound.
- **E:** Comprises a minor 2nd degree, giving melodies a Middle-Eastern sound.

The B natural note scale comprises a minor third. However, it also has a diminished 5th, making it difficult to work with.

Relative Minor and Major

Both the A natural minor and C major use the same notes. Creating a minor or major scale requires that the notes be centered around a specific tonic. When major and natural minor scales share the same 7 notes, they are known as the relative major and relative minor.

Look at the harmonica scales with minor or major characters. You will see the following:

- **A:** C's relative minor
- **D:** F's relative minor
- **E:** G's relative minor

When you learn and understand these relationships, you can learn to play songs that switch between the relative major and minor keys and chords.

Playing Minor Keys on Diatonic Harmonicas

While harmonicas can be tuned in minor keys, most musicians tend to use major-key harmonicas and play the minor keys by choosing a scale containing a minor 3rd degree. For example, you could play a C harmonica in A, D, or E minor.

Modal Scales

Any note in a scale can be designated the tonic, and the resulting scales are called modes. In a seven-note scale, there are seven modes or modal scales. Most scale step patterns are a mixture of semitones and whole tones, meaning the modes have different interval qualities.

You will also find D, E, F, G, A, and B modal scales on a C-tuned diatonic harmonica. Each provides the basis for playing the same harmonica in different keys.

We'll look at the major, major pentatonic, minor, minor pentatonic, and blues scales, working in the first, second, and third positions.

Scales are series of notes following a pattern. The intervals between those notes determine the pattern. If you swap patterns, you are changing to a different scale, and you'll get a different feel to it. This enables you to get new ideas.

Playing a scale may be easier in one position than another, and below, you'll see we choose the right position for the scales.

Playing these scales requires you to be able to play single, clean notes, but you should already know how to do that.

Scales in First Position

The 1st position begins on blow holes 1 and 4, 7, and 10. It provides the same key as the one the harmonica is tuned in, i.e., key C for a C-tuned harmonica. This is the best position for major scales, playing happy songs and bright melodies.

Major Pentatonic Scale:

4 -4 5 6 -6 7

Full Major Scale:

4 -4 5 -5 6 -6 -7 7

Ionian Mode:

4 -4 5 -5 6 -6 -7 7

Scales in Second Position

The 2nd position begins on draw hole 2 and blow holes 6 and 9. It is a fifth up from the key the harmonica is tuned in, for example, key G on a C-tuned harmonica. It is the best position for blues songs, exploring the tension between minor and major keys and using the Mixolydian mode.

Major Pentatonic Scale:

-2 -3// -3 -4 5 6

Full Major Scale:

-2 -3// -3 4 -4 5 5* 6

Minor Pentatonic Scale:

-2 -3/ 4 -4 -5 6

The Blues Scale:

-2 -3/ 4 -4/ -4 -5 6

Mixolydian Mode:

-2 -3// -3 4 -4 5 -5 6

(or: 6 -6 -7 7 -8 8 -9 9)

The blues scale is basically an extra note added to the minor pentatonic. This means the minor pentatonic is typically used in blues, rock, and many other musical styles.

Scales in Third Position

The third position begins on draw holes 1, 4, and 8 and is two semitones above the key the harmonica is tuned in, for example, key D on a C-tuned harmonica. It is the best position to play the Dorian mode, minor scales and to produce expressive bending. It isn't commonly used in major scales, but it can be.

Major Pentatonic Scale:

-1 2 -2/ -3// -3 -4

Full Major Scale:

-1 2 -2/ -2 -3// -3 -4/ -4

Minor Pentatonic Scale:

-1 -2// -2 -3// 4 -4

The Blues Scale:

-1 -2// -2 -3/// -3// 4 -4

Natural Minor Scale:

-1 2 -2// -2 -3// -3/ 4 -4

Dorian Mode:

-1 2 -2// -2 -3// -3 4 -4

(or: -4 5 -5 6 -6 -7 7 -8)

The blues and minor pentatonic can be played in 2nd and 3rd positions, so experiment and see which works for you.

Practicing Scales Properly

Some beginner players seem to be scared of playing scales, but they are one of the best tools to help you use music to express your feelings. They should not be considered a barrier; they are a bridge to help you learn to play emotively and expressively.

But Why Do You Need to Practice Them?

For the three reasons listed below:

1. When you can move up and down the scales, your technique improves, and you will find it easier to move up and down the harmonica easily and smoothly.

2. You can incorporate the scale in your music.

3. Lastly, practicing the scales helps you see what you play.

As with anything, consistent practice is the only way to improve. Once you master scales, you can experiment with them to produce your own unique style.

Chapter 7: Advanced Techniques

It's time to look at a couple of advanced techniques. While they may be advanced, they are crucial techniques in learning to play the harmonica as your favorite musicians do. Those two techniques are bending and vibrato.

Bending

You've heard that wonderful bluesy sound being played on the harmonica, but how do you replicate it on your harmonica? The secret to that is in bending. If you can master bending, you can put soul into any song you play, something you can't do when you only play single notes.

So, what is bending, and what's the point in learning it?

Harmonica bending allows you to lower a note's pitch, and there are two great reasons why you should learn it:

1. To make your music expressive. Bending is a great technique that emulates the human voice. In

particular, it can emulate the wailing sounds we associate with bluesy, soulful harmonica music.

2. To play missing notes. A harmonica is only capable of so many notes, but with bending, you can access many more. Some of those are the blue notes we use in playing blues music, but it will take mastery to learn how to do it, even to play the major scale in a lower octave, i.e., in the first to fourth holes.

How to Bend

You need to learn two techniques to master bending, both related to one another. I don't want you to try this yet; just read through it. The steps will be explained further in a while.

1. **Activate the Bend:** Be aware that it can take you weeks, if not months, to master this. You do it by:

- Positioning the back of your tongue in the Kk zone. This is the closest part of your palate to your pharynx.

- Inhaling some air so it goes between your palate and tongue.

- Moving the Kk zone forward and backward until you hear the pitch drop.

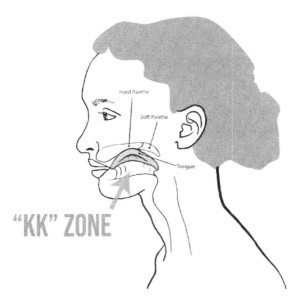

Hard Palette

Soft Palette

Tongue

"KK" ZONE

18. Be aware that it can take you weeks, if not months, to master the bending technique. Source: https://www.harmonica.com/wp-content/uploads/2020/12/Kea-Image-1-The-Kk-Zone-edited-scaled.jpg

This might sound simple, but it will take time to perfect it. Practice makes perfect

2. **Adjust the Bend:** Tuning the oral cavity will help you master getting sound from the bend, but it depends on the tone you want to achieve:

- Bend deeper to get a lower pitch. Move your tongue away from the Kk zone as far as you can and lift your soft palate. Open the back of your throat to do this.

- Shrink your mouth to reduce the height of the bend. Bring the back of your tongue down, away from the Kk zone, and relax your throat at the back.

This will all make sense to you shortly.

Prerequisites

Before you can even think about bending, you must be proficient at the deep, relaxed mouth position. This allows you to play single notes and is done like this:

1. Hold your harmonica with the first hole on the left and the tenth on the right.

2. Lick your lips to wet them. Relax your lips and position the harmonica into your mouth.

3. Turn the harmonica a little, ensuring that the section not touched by your lips is facing the ceiling. It should be at a rough 30-degree angle.

4. Keep your top lip relaxed and the harmonica deep inside it.

5. This is a very important step – allow your lower lip to unfold until the moist inner part touches the harmonica. Use the fingers on the hand, not holding the harmonica to pull your lip down to achieve this.

6. If your position is correct, the harmonica should feel a little deeper inside the top lip than the bottom one.

You must also be sure that you can use lip blocking to play single notes. Both techniques will make sure that you have the correct seal for bending.

You will need no small amount of patience here. For a while, you will feel like you can't get the hang of bending; you might achieve it once and then struggle for a long time afterward. Allow yourself several days, if not weeks, to get the hang of this, and expect it to take longer to master.

Don't push yourself too hard, and make sure you take a lot of breaks. Start by practicing for a few minutes, but be consistent. Trying too hard or practicing too long will make your attempts to learn much harder.

Your First Bend

Breathe in deeply and relax. Remember not to try too hard. We will look at several ways for you to achieve your first bend, so don't get upset if you don't get it right the first time.

The Kk Zone

This is an important approach because it can help get your first bend activated and will later help you tune it. Right now, your focus should be on achieving a bend; forget about trying to get it in tune.

Most players learn to bend the -4 hole on the C harmonica first. However, some will achieve a -1 bend before the -4. The two recommendations below will help you see in which order to do it:

- Mostly on -4.

- If you struggle, try it on -1.

You need to understand where the back of your tongue hits the roof of your mouth on the hard palate. Say Kk repeatedly until you can feel it. This is the Kk zone. Ignoring your harmonica for the minute, inhale while your tongue stays in the Kk zone.

This zone allows suction between the roof of your mouth and tongue and can be moved forward or backward. Be aware that you do not really move the tip of your tongue.

Learning to play with this will help you achieve and fine-tune your bends. Let's get a feel for this. Make a sound like an airplane diving down, keeping your tongue in the zone. Listen to how it sounds and the feeling you get on your soft palate and back of your throat. Make the same noise while you inhale, feeling how your tongue moves.

Now, you can try it on the -4 hole on your harmonica.

If it doesn't work, have a go on the -1 hole.

The latter requires keeping the Kk zone far back and lifting your soft palate.

The Tilt Bend

Some say you need to change the jet stream direction in your mouth to activate a bend. If that's the case, it goes some way toward explaining why the tilt bend works, and it could be the way you get your first successful bend.

As you bend your pitch down, tilt the harmonica at a roughly 45-degree angle so the front of it moves toward the ceiling.

EE-YAW

If that doesn't work, try this. Vocalize the vowels ee through aw. Your mouth should be wide on ee, while on aw, it should be open at the back and tall. As you inhale while vocalizing them, try to see the pitch dropping as you say them on -4.

KAH-YOO

Try this if you still haven't been successful. Say Kah and then say, Yoo. As you do, the Y sound should be emphasized, channeling through the Kk zone. Try saying it as you inhale, then try it on hole -4 with the harmonica.

How to Tell if You Are Bending Correctly

When you first start learning this, you might struggle to hear if the pitch drops when you try bending a note. Because of that, you won't know if you have been successful. You can download harmonica bending tools to your phone or tablet or look online for free bending tools.

Here are some tips to help you:

1. Are You Passing through the Bend?

Some beginners try for weeks to learn to bend and get so frustrated that they can't do it. In most cases, they are actually achieving the bend, but because they get the bend and release it quickly, they can't hear it. Slow the movement as you move the back of your tongue toward the back of your mouth. And learn to listen. If necessary, record yourself and play it back.

2. Try to Visualize the Dropping Pitch

Yes, I get that this sounds weird, but bending a note on your harmonica is nothing more than tuning your mouth cavity to a slightly lower pitch than the pitch the harmonica bends to. Try to hear the pitch as it drops; this can help you successfully bend a note.

3. Try to Relax

The commonest thing that stops beginners from success is tension. The more frustrated you get, the more tense you get.

Stop what you are doing, breathe deeply, and relax. Before you start, say to yourself, "I don't care if I succeed in learning to bend; it really isn't that big a deal," and you'll instantly put yourself in the right frame of mind.

4. Keep Trying

There's a good chance you haven't succeeded yet. If you have, great. Well done! If not, please keep trying. Go back to the beginning and start over, slowly following everything. Then put it away and go do something else. Come back and have another go. The trick is not to overdo or make your practice sessions too long. It will come to you eventually and probably when you least expect it.

Playing Riffs

When you finally get the hang of the bend and can do it fairly consistently, put it into practice on some real tunes.

Doobie Brothers: Long Train Runnin'

If you learned the -4 bend, you can start with the harmonica solo in the Doobie Brothers' "Long Train Runnin'."

As you can see below, it begins going up into -4, bending and releasing.

-4 -4" -4

So, that's really what you have been practicing through this whole chapter. Draw hole 4, bend down, and release it.

Then, there are three small scoops:

-4" -4 -4" -4 -4" -4

Later in the song, you'll hear the lead vocalist play some difficult rhythms, but we don't need to worry about learning those fast. The trick is to take your time and learn each step slowly and carefully.

Before you can get into difficult rhythms, you need to understand how a note starts in the bent position.

Play the note and then bend it down. Immediately stop the airflow while concentrating on the inside of your mouth. You mustn't let anything change in there. Let the airflow start again, and repeat. Continue repeating until you can do this consistently and correctly every time. When you can do it, repeat the following riff as many times as you want to practice:

-4" -4 -4

Over time, you will learn to play this riff faster, and when you do, it might benefit you to articulate "Toe-ah" on the draw bend note, release it, and follow it with a "Ta" syllable on the last note.

Toe - ah Ta

-' -4 -4 (repeat over and over)

Deep Purple: Smoke on the Water

You can try this song when you are proficient at starting a note in the bent position. In this, we'll focus on bending -6. Do this in much the same way as you did -4 but a bit more forward and smaller in the mouth:

-4 -5 6 -4 -5 -6" 6   -4 -5 6 -5

This was originally recorded in the G key, so to play along with the actual recording, you need a harmonic tuned in low F.

John Denver: Take Me Home Country Roads

This is a simple song, but you can spice it up with a couple of bends. The original tablature is:

4 -4 5 5 4 -4 5 -4 4 5 6 -6

The last note in the 2nd and 4th phrases is our target for bending:

4 -4 5 5 4 -4" -4 5 -4 4 5 6 -6" -6

This is played in the A key, so you need an A harmonica if you want to play along with the actual recording.

Are you happy with your progress? Bending is a fantastic technique that, once learned, can help you add so much more to your music.

Bending Tips:

If you are struggling to get this right, try the following tips:

- **Whistle Backwards:** Bending is much like changing a whistle's pitch, so have a go at it without using the harmonica. Pay close attention to yourself while you do it. Start by whistling a high note and slide it down. If you can, try it as you inhale. Transfer your tongue and mouth movement to the harmonica when you think you've got it.

- **Freeze:** One of the most crucial things to getting the bend right is keeping your embouchure consistent. If you do manage to move the note, freeze your mouth in that exact position and try to memorize it. You'll need to work at this - watching yourself in a mirror can help. Even the slightest movement can mean failure.

- **Think Lower:** If you think the note is lower, it really can help. There is a connection between the note you achieve and your vocal cavity. If you think lower, you will unconsciously move your embouchure so it's in the right shape.

- **Start Your Car:** Not literally, just imagine that you are doing it. Those who drive manual cars must learn to find the biting point by balancing the gas and clutch. This is what allows you to move the car smoothly away. Bends have much the same biting point; miss it, and you won't achieve the bend. Listen and learn to recognize when that point occurs. When you get it, pause, and the bend will be maintained.

Common Bending Mistakes

You'll succeed quickly with any luck, but most beginners don't. That might be because you are making one of the common mistakes:

- **Your Breath Is Too Hard.** If something isn't working, many people believe the way to fix it is to force it. In this case, you need to do the complete opposite. Relax, loosen up, and steady yourself with a few deep breaths. Focus on finding that biting point, but don't overdo your practice session.

- **You Rush the Changes.** Trying to do everything too quickly – your mouth, tongue, and air pressure – can lead to you missing the bend. Slow down, as if you were playing in slow motion, you'll have more success.

- **You Aren't Using the Right Harmonica.** If you buy a cheap harmonica, you can't expect much from it.

If you get one free with a learning book, it won't work. You have to use a good-quality harmonica if you want to use it to its full potential.

Vibrato

The other advanced technique you should learn is vibrato, which can make your music sound more expressive and mature and add texture. It isn't easy to learn, but, like anything, consistent practice will help you.

Pulsating Notes

Playing a sustained note and steadily pulsating it is vibrato. Gentle pulses are used on a note to gently ripple it within the sound you are sustaining. This is done the same way you stop and start notes but gentler.

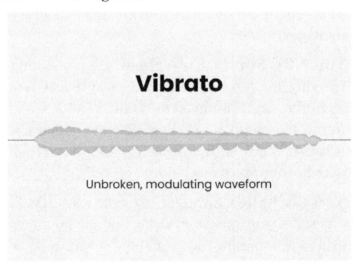

19. Gentle pulses are used on a note to gently ripple it within the sound you are sustaining. Source: https://www.harpsurgery.com/how-to-play/vibrato/

You can produce this in three ways on your harmonica:

1. Raise the note's pitch and dip it down to just below the normal pitch. This is how string instrument players do it, and many experienced harmonica players will tell you this is the only way to create a true vibrato.

2. Vary the note's pitch.

3. Changing the tone's color between dark and bright.

The Diaphragm Vibrato

This kind of vibrato changes the pitch without changing the note's tone, color, or pitch. As you inhale and exhale, bounce your diaphragm. However, you don't articulate the individual notes in a series. Instead, your breath must be sustained between each diaphragm bounce, resulting in a continuous pulsating sound.

Follow these steps to do it:

1. Breathe in deeply.

2. As you begin to breathe out, thrust your abdomen out.

3. Continue breathing out with several consistent gentle thrusts. Do not allow your breath to stop flowing at any time.

You should hear what sounds like a long note with even pulses throughout.

Now try it using your harmonica:

1. Play the draw and blow notes in hole 4.

2. Make sure that each note is held long enough for the vibrato to happen.

The Throat Vibrato

This type of vibrato can change a note's pitch and loudness.

When you use your glottis to pulse the note, the airflow doesn't stop, but your air passage does become smaller. This vibrato doesn't sound the same as when you do it with abdominal thrusts. Throat vibrato adds a throb to the sound rather than a ripple.

Try these steps to have a go at it.

1. First, whisper the following in one breath – "!Ah!Ah!Ah!Ah!Ah!" Every" exclamation mark is one glottal stop.

2. Do this silently and gently, aiming for an uninterrupted continuous airflow.

3. Next, try it with your harmonica. Blow into it, using your glottis to keep the note sounding continuously. At the same time, use your glottis to massage the air into pulses.

All the while, your abdominal movements should be smooth, with no pulsing. This one is all done in the throat, nowhere else.

The Tongue Vibrato

You can use the tongue vibrato to alter a note's pitch and tone color. To practice it, follow these steps:

1. To prepare yourself, say the following in one breath: " Ung-Ung-Ung-Ung."

2. As the ng sound is made, you find the section of your tongue halfway back raises, stopping the airflow.

3. Now try to raise it yourself, but not so much that it stops the airflow.

4. You should hear a sound similar to "Ayayayaya." The y comes from your tongue as it raises, and there are a few things you should notice about its sound:

- As your tongue raises, the sound should be brighter.

- You should hear the sound of a slight air hiss, sounding somewhere between y and g.

- You should feel the air pressure holding your tongue down so it doesn't touch the roof of your mouth.

5. The next step is to try the same with your harmonica.

6. Try creating a subtle pulse without changing the vowel sound too much.

You should use the air pressure you feel when using this on blow notes to develop the pitch. And, when draw notes are played, raising your tongue will create suction, which should be used to drive the pitch change.

The Hand Vibrato

Using your hand to create the vibrato can change a note's pitch. The more movement there is in the hand that isn't holding the harmonica, the stronger the tone color change. Swing your elbow if you want a vibrato with a lot of color, but be aware that while this sounds good in some musical pieces, it won't suit everything.

There are three types of hand vibrato:

Squeeze

1. Enclose the harmonica completely in both hands.

2. Play a note and sustain it. At the same time, press the hand not holding the harmonica slightly into the one that is.

3. Release the pressure, but do not open your hands – the harmonica must remain enclosed.

4. Repeat, noting the pulsating sound you create.

Pinkie

1. Again, enclose your harmonica entirely and play a sustained note.

2. Raise your pinkie finger on the hand, not holding the harmonica, creating a small gap between your hands.

3. Raise and lower it and listen to the pulsating sound.

Wrist Rock

1. Enclose the harmonica again and play a sustained note.

2. Rock the wrist on the hand, not holding the harmonica, opening up a small gap between your hands. You can do this by opening your palms at the edges or making the gap between the heels of your palms.

3. The more opening gap there is, the bigger the tone change.

Master this, and it can help you create many different pulsing sounds.

As you practice, move your hand slowly and carefully; you should be able to hear when the note's volume goes up. Use that point to center your vibrato, and you can vary the pitch at the same time.

Chapter 8: Improvisation and Jamming

When you learn to play an instrument like the harmonica, you might get bored of straightforward playing. Now that your ears are trained, and you've got great listening skills, listen to some of your favorite musicians, not particularly their released recordings but some of their concerts. You might notice that some songs sound different, and that's because the musician has improvised in certain areas.

However, improvisation isn't just about playing what you want, even though the definition of improvising is:

"Create and perform (music, verse, discourse, etc.), spur of the moment, unrehearsed, without preparation or meditation, composing music mentally in the same act of performing it."

The words "without preparation" don't mean not being prepared when it comes to improvisation. It simply refers to unplanned music that you think of and play. Improvising is an important part of harmonica playing, but it has to be prepared for.

20. *Improvising is an important part of harmonica playing, but it has to be prepared for. Source: https://www.pexels.com/photo/woman-in-white-shirt-holding-pen-writing-on-white-paper-4709832/*

Learning to Improvise

Learning to improvise is about technique, but it takes more than that. Some musicians can play any piece of music you put before them, but they have no clue how to improvise. Why not? Well, improvisation requires patience, time, practice, and a reason to do it. Learning to improvise can bring great satisfaction. It can also be a kind of "rescue remedy" if something goes wrong during your performance. Aside from performances where you must perform the exact music, improvisation gives you the freedom to play with confidence so that if you do forget your notes, you can fill in with something else.

The rest of this chapter is dedicated to tips on improvisation and jamming, another great way to learn improvisation and get some practice.

1. **Consider Improvisation Being Like Talking.** Your harmonica is your voice, and you use it to speak. If you wanted to become a truly great storyteller, you would benefit from reading different genres. The same applies to improvisation. The more you study, the better your voice will be. Study a wide range of rhythms and musical genres, and your musical language will soon improve.

2. **You Need a Good Technical Background.** Some musicians and music lovers argue against this, but it's a fact. Shaping your improvisation requires technique. While much improvisation comes from the heart and soul, you cannot express it without the right technical ability. If you cannot visualize your goal, how can you play it? Instead, it will stay an idea in your mind and never become a reality.

3. **Use the Right Tools.** Some things are required for improvisation. Make blues scales, minor scales, major scales, pentatonic scales, patterns, and arpeggios part of your daily life. At the end of

the day, every musical piece, every passage in every piece, has its roots in one of these, and they are your building blocks.

4. **Set Progressions.** By this, I mean take your time bringing all your ideas out. Remember that improvisation is like talking. Instead of gabbling everything you want to say at once, build it up slowly. Use simple elements to start with and add to them gradually. Here are some techniques you can use:

- Begin with short phrases that only contain a few notes. As you advance, increase your intensity.

- Start with the harmonica's low end and gradually move to the higher notes. These add tension to your music.

- Get your emotions across by using dynamics. These work on the sensations listeners feel when listening to a piece of music.

    1. **Use Pauses.** Pauses are a part of music, adding one between phrases allows the listeners to understand what you said with your music. This is effective, so train yourself to add pauses in single melodic lines and between two phrases.

    2. **Play What You Think.** Think of two notes in a sequence and play them one after the other. Then go to three, four, and more notes – think them first, then play them. Eventually, you will be playing more complex pieces. The trick is to be able to hum the line you want to play and then play it on your harmonica at any given time.

3. **Think of Your Vision.** Where do you want to start? Where do you want to go regarding phrasing, dynamics, and note height? Imagine a dialogue between two or three people or a monologue, and play it so your listeners understand who is talking.

4. **Get into Battle with Other Musicians.** Get a group of musicians together, and each plays two, four, or eight bars, alternating between players. That's a great way to learn to improvise, making jamming sessions worth it.

5. **Learn Using the Best Tool You Have.** It's with you always, wherever you go: your mind. Hum out loud or in your mind. The more you do it, the more skilled you will become, and you'll soon be improvising with the best of them.

6. **Go Easy.** When you improvise, you are not firing a machine gun! You don't need to fire notes out all over the place. Say anything with your harmonica, but not so much that you sound like a gossipy old lady (or man!)

Let's move on to some more practical tips:

1. **Rhythmic Improvisation:** Forget getting too complicated. First, keep it simple by picking a single note and learning to improvise with it. Start with drawing hole 2. You can use whichever rhythm you want.

2. **Using a 12-Bar Blues Rhythm, Follow the Chord Changes**. This is a continuation of the

above tip. The root notes from the I, IV, and V chords correspond to the draw hole 2, blow hole 4, and draw hole 4. Rhythmically improvise these holes using the root notes of those chords. So, you only play draw hole 2 on the I chord, blow hole 4 on the IV chord, and 4 hole draw on the V chord. Use whichever rhythm you want.

3. **Use the Blues Scale**. Pretty much every blues solo is based on this scale, so you need to know it inside out. Choose two or three notes from the scale and experiment with them to create your own phrase.

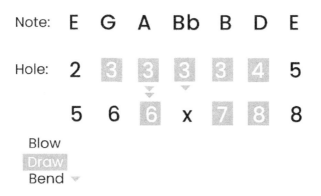

Blues Scale (Fifth Position):

21. *Pretty much every blues solo is based on this scale, so you need to know it inside out. Source: https://content.instructables.com/FJN/H003/GAPV2UPX/FJNH0 03GAPV2UPX.jpg?auto=webp&fit=bounds&frame=1&height=1024 &width=1024auto=webp&frame=1&height=150*

4. **Learn Phrases from Other Players**. One of the easiest ways to learn is to start by copying the best players. Choose a recording, choose one phrase from it, and listen to it. Try to work out what it is by ear, but be prepared to pause and rewind the piece a lot! It takes practice, but the more you do it, the better you will be. Eventually, you will hear it in your mind and be able to play it on your harmonica.

5. **Build One Phrase into a 12-Bar Phrase.** In the same way that a conversation has a theme, so should a blues solo. You could just play a whole load of phrases, but it won't sound cohesive and will lack passion. One of the best strategies is to use a phrase in a 12-bar sequence. Don't use it the same way all the time; change it up each time you play the sequence. Create different variations, changing the chord tone, response, etc. The idea is to learn to improvise by putting that phrase into a bar anywhere, at any time. You could even make it more difficult by using two phrases.

When in Doubt

Finally, we have a few simple tips to help you when jamming blues, harmonica, and other musical genres.

First, a quick shortcut for beginners using a set of notes in the second position to start jamming.

Here's the Almost Blues Scale:

3B 3D   4B

4D 5D   6B

To make your own riffs, use any one of these notes or all of them. Do not start on blow hole 4. It will also sound better if you end on blow hole 3 or 6. When you know what you want to do, repeat it a few times so it feels like a melody. Forget about adding other techniques to start with. And don't worry if your single notes aren't perfect; a bit of sloppiness adds to the improvisation.

Let's get onto those jamming shortcuts and tips:

1. Use draw holes 2 and 4 when jamming in the second position in a simple style, especially if you are playing a blues harp. Bending, sliding, hand effects, and other basic methods can be used to create riffs. Use blow hole 3 and keep working on draw hole 2 if you're having trouble with that one. Add it back in after that.

2. Use long-held notes at any tempo, whether slow, medium, or fast, when you're unsure what to play rhythmically. Make those notes sound interesting by adding hand effects, harsh and soft dynamics, and bending.

3. When jamming in the first position, focus mostly on the middle blow notes.

4. Ask someone when you can't work out the key a song you are jamming is in. Experienced players will always know.

5. When you can't decide if you are playing too much or not enough while in a jamming session, opt for playing less. If you want to be asked back to the session, ensure the other players have space to

play and the singer can be heard. When the singer stops singing, play in the blank spaces. Try not to play while they sing and stop when they do sing – it irritates them when you don't do this. If you must play while they are singing, stick to simple chords and riffs and play them softly.

6. When you struggle to know what to play, just keep it simple. Stick with what you know. Don't try to play stuff you've only been working on for the last couple of weeks. You don't know enough about it yet to have mastered it. Repeating straightforward riffs will give your music a pleasant melody.

7. When you can't understand how to make your second position sound more bluesy, bend more notes on the draw holes 2 and 4.

8. By the same token, you can give your music a country feel in the second position by bending more on draw hole 3.

9. Learn the third position and use it to play music written in a minor key.

10. Don't waste too much time thinking. Just close your eyes, go with the flow, and enjoy yourself.

11. Licking your lips beforehand will prevent them from being glued to the harp. As often as necessary, repeat.

12. To get rid of extra saliva, rap your harmonica against your palm or leg with the mouthpiece pointing down. This will prevent the holes from clogging. Repeat as often as necessary.

13. Take a few minutes to get up and work on your posture and breathing. As you stand, keep your head high, your shoulders back, and your back straight.

Chapter 9: Playing Amplified

You've listened to your favorite players, even watched them in concert, and now you want to amplify your sound like they do. You're ready to go out and splurge on all the gear.

Stop.

Before you do that, pick up your harp and play it for half an hour or so. Do you like it? Does your tone please you? If not, you need to work on that BEFORE you splash out on expensive mics and amplifiers. The sound you play is what gets amplified – much louder – and if you don't like it now, you won't like it then.

If you do like what you hear and are happy with your sound and playing style, you'll need two main pieces of equipment – a microphone and an amplifier. And your harmonica, obviously. These all work together to produce the amplified sound you will hear. The final result is your sound, and it is probably 80% of your acoustic tone. That's why you need to sound good before you can even think of going amplified.

Another 10% of that tone comes from the cup between your hand, microphone, and face. Getting that 80% is almost impossible if you don't have a decent seal on the cup.

22. Master the basics before you amplify your sound. Source: https://unsplash.com/photos/SP9HcRASMPE

Amps

First, a safety warning. The levels of voltage in an amplifier are lethal, so please do not mess around with the inside them unless you are qualified to do so. Some people still use old vintage amps, and you can still buy them, but not all have been grounded properly. It's not uncommon to hear of players being electrocuted when they use these amps.

If you purchase an old amp, get a qualified person to ensure it is grounded and safe to use. If necessary, take it to a professional technician who can check it out and fix it up for you.

There's a huge range of amplifiers if you play a keyboard or guitar, but very few specifically for the harmonica. Those that are available are expensive, more than $1,000. However, new isn't always the best choice for getting the right sound where the harmonica is concerned. You want that old 1940s Chicago Blues sound, the era that gave us some of the best harmonica players in the world – Little Walter, Big Walter Horton, and both Sonny Boy Williamson. That sound can only be achieved by using the old-fashioned bullet-type mic and tube amplifier.

The Fender tube amps that come from the late 1950s through the early 1960s are the most sought-after, with the most popular being the 1959 Fender Bassman. In fact, their popularity has grown so much Fender has started producing a Re-Issue (RI) Bassman tube amp again. Many harmonica players use this because it offers the right volume and sound to compete with other instrument players, particularly the guitar player, in reasonably large venues.

Settings

The hardest part is getting the amp set up right to give you the sound you want. How you do it will depend on the amp you buy, together with your mic, environment, and what you want to achieve.

However, here are a few things you need to consider:

- The tone controls cannot be changed independently. Unlike a home stereo system where, when you change one tone control on your amp, all the others are affected, too. So, to get your sound right, you need to adjust them all together. All amps are different. Even those of the same model will have different requirements to get your sound right.

- The bass must be emphasized. The bass controls are usually turned more than halfway up. When you add bass, it makes the sound seem fuller and more rounded. However, because the tone controls depend on one another, you will need to get to grips with the settings on your amp to ensure that the bass is emphasized. You might find you need the bass to be lower than the treble to get the sound you want.

- The treble should be toned down, with the emphasis taken off it. The treble controls are usually turned more than halfway down. When you add treble, it adds a cutting, brittle, sharp sound that often results in the worst feedback possible.

- Mid-range is usually de-emphasized, but this can vary a lot.

- You will normally find the reverb setting around halfway up, normally low to moderate.

- Gain controls are used to set the total volume in conjunction with the master volume controls but also to work out what distortion you have. More gain results in more overdrive, leading to more volume and distortion. To make the sound louder, turn the master volume up. To maintain the volume but remove distortion, turn the volume up and gain down. The volume should be turned up, and the gain turned down for a cleaner sound.

Microphones

Apart from an amp, you need a microphone, and, in the same way as for amplifiers, plenty of them are available, new and vintage. One of the biggest factors determining the sound a mic produces is the element, and you can choose from several, including dynamic, crystal, controlled magnetic, and ceramic.

One of the best mics to use with tube amps is the Green Bullet. It has a dynamic element, although older ones may have different ones and a distortion type that many players want to help them round out their sound. The Astatic JT30 contains a crystal element, giving tube distortion a classic edge or bite.

23. One of the best mics to use with tube amps is the Green Bullet.
Source: Ky, CC BY 2.0
<https://creativecommons.org/licenses/by/2.0>, via Wikimedia Commons:
https://commons.wikimedia.org/wiki/File:Shure_520DX_Green_Bullet_-
_Dynamic_Harmonica_Microphone,_along_with_microphone_vo lume_knob_on_Gibson_Kalamazoo_amplifier_model_KEH-....jpg

Some players use more than one microphone, and many will search for a long time to find the perfect one, in the same way they look for the best amp. The trick is to find both at the same time. Some combos work together better than others do. Because the most important part of the mic is the element, two mics that seem identical but have different elements can produce completely different sounds. Many players will search hard to find the element that suits them best.

Some players won't worry about an amp and will play through a PA system at a venue. In that case, they choose PA mics, such as the Shure SM-57 or SM-58. PA mics are good for amplifying acoustic play or when a musician plays with little overdriven distortion, a clean sound, in other words. You don't hold it in your hand when you use a mic for acoustic playing. Instead, you place it on a stand at least a foot away from your harmonica. Some players will change their distance, starting by cupping the mic, moving away, and going back again, providing their sound with variety.

If you use a smaller mic, you stand a better chance of getting an airtight cup, plus it gives you more range of hand effects. You can purchase battery-powered tie-clip mics like the Radio Shack Optimus 33-3013. These are good for a microphone that uses standard hand techniques for acoustic playing, but they don't offer the characteristic distortion many players seek. You can even use cheaper cassette recorder mics, which work okay for amplified harmonica. This is because they have a limited dynamic range, which suits the harmonica well. They are good for practicing with and work fine with the mini amps you might use for practice, but you wouldn't use them when playing professionally.

One mic that is specifically designed for use with the harmonica is the Strnad mic, as it has a sealed plastic cup to hold the instrument. They offer a clean sound, and you can use them to amplify harmonicas placed in a neck rack, for example, when you play your harmonica with a guitar simultaneously.

Effects

Effects used on guitars can be used on a harmonica, although, typically, amplified harmonicas rely on a smaller set of effects. The most common ones are delay and reverb.

You won't often use distortion effects as they add too much unpleasant-sounding distortion and way too much feedback. You will often find reverb already built into your amplifier, or you can purchase an external reverb tank.

The delay effect provides the sound with varying amounts of echo. For example, you would normally only use a small amount of delay to simulate playing in a medium-sized room or empty hall. That said, lengths of delay can be changed between short and very long. While you can buy digital delay pedals, many prefer analog versions.

How to Hold the Harmonica and Mic

When you first play a harmonica amplified, you will likely use a mic plugged into a sound system. It will typically be a vocal mic used for singing, which is fine because they work well for harmonicas.

Mics on a Stand

When you use a mic connected to a sound system, the mic is normally on a stand. This is to ensure it is at the right height and distance for a singer.

- **Adjust the Stand.** The end of the mic must be at the same height as your mouth. You don't want to stand up on your toes or crouch down, which will not be comfortable, and your audience will wonder what you are doing.

- **Positioning the Microphone.** If you want the best sound pickup, make sure the microphone is pointed straight towards the sound source. If you are holding your harmonica, the sound is coming from the back of your hands. If a neck rack is being used, it is the back of the harmonica.

- **Find the Right Position.** Get as close to the microphone as you can to get the best sound out of it. If you hear a loud howling noise, you have feedback; move back until it stops.

- **Have Enough Space for Your Hands.** How you hold the acoustic harmonica in your hands has a significant impact on the sound you produce. Your hands produce a brilliant sound when they are cupped and a dark one when they are uncupped. Alternating creates a "wah" impression. To avoid hitting the microphone, make sure that your hands have enough space.

Your first time using a stand might not be appropriate. You might just be equipped with a microphone to use when performing. In that scenario, you must have the necessary skills.

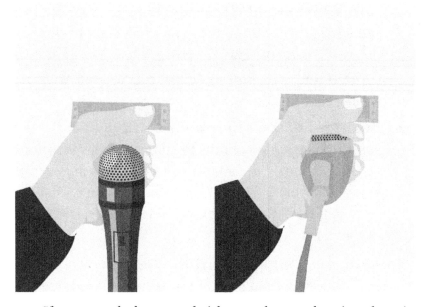

24. If you want the best sound pickup, make sure the microphone is pointed straight towards the sound source. Source: https://www.dummies.com/wp-content/uploads/456302.image1.jpg

Cupping the Mic in Your Hands

Often, harmonica players will cup the mic and harmonica together to give a natural harmonica sound that is more concentrated and stronger.

These advantages come your way when you cup the mic in this manner:

- Other instruments, especially loud ones like electric guitars and drums, won't be audible through your microphone.

- You get a louder sound than if the mic weren't cupped.

- You can move around the stage, and your sound will still be heard because the microphone follows you.

- It may also have additional effects, some of which you might not want:

- You will be less able to sculpt tone with your hands because the microphone is now situated where your hands would typically create an acoustic sound chamber.

- It is less common to pronounce words before loud and gentle sounds.

- The sound of your harmonica will alter. Because the higher frequencies are less audible, your music will appear darker and more mellow.

If a sound technician is present, alert them if you're about to cup a microphone in your hands. So that no one's ears are harmed by the noise, the volume needs to be lowered. Failure to lower the microphone may cause speaker damage due to feedback or loud harmonica noises.

A finger's width should separate your harp from the microphone. You won't continue to play the harp loudly into the microphone. As a result, you also obtain a tone chamber. By altering the cup's configuration around the mic, you can use the chamber to produce tonal effects.

Listening to Yourself

When you first play on stage, it could be difficult for you to hear your own sounds as well as those of the other musicians. This might be a result of background noise from the audience, powerful amplifiers, and the distance between you and the other performers. You risk playing the incorrect notes if you cannot hear yourself when playing the harmonica.

However, a competent sound system will almost certainly have monitors. These are little speakers that are angled upward and placed on the floor so you can hear your sound. Ask the sound engineer if they can perform a sound check for you if you have the time.

If you are unable to hear yourself, you can either:

- **Request a Louder Monitor Volume.** To indicate to the sound technician that you require a louder monitor, first point to your ear and then up.

- **Insert Your Finger into Your Ear**. Sticking your finger in your ear can help you hear your sound, but this is a last resort.

You can feel overpowered by the loud noise on the stage. You might then blow too much air into the harmonica as a result. Do not abuse the harmonica by bashing it up, screaming, or honking. You'll sound better if you play at your usual volume and properly control your harmonica.

How to Avoid Howling Feedback

Feedback can be excruciatingly loud, filling the space with a wailing sound. This occurs when audio is captured by the mic, played back via the speaker, and then captured by the mic once more before being played back through the audio system.

The following situations should be avoided at all costs because they could lead to it:

- If the microphone is directly facing the speakers or gets too close to them

- If your amplifier is playing too loud. Any direction you point the microphone in this situation will take up sound.

- When certain frequencies are amplified in a hollow space, they ring and produce feedback.

Chapter 10: Care and Maintenance of Your Harmonica

Although harmonicas look simply constructed, can easily be carried in your pocket, and are intuitive to play, there is so much more to the instrument than that. Whether you play a diatonic or chromatic harmonica, forgetting how sensitive and delicate they are is easy because most of the workmanship is on the inside. And sometimes your sliders will jam, and your reeds will go out of key, which takes the fun out of playing.

Most of the time, issues like this will have nothing to do with how the harmonica was made or whether it goes wrong. No, mostly, they are down to a lack of maintenance, which must be done to ensure your harmonica plays as it should and lasts as long as possible.

This chapter is dedicated to everything you must do to care for and maintain your harmonica before, during, and after you play it.

1. Reminder about the Different Parts

It doesn't matter which make or model your harmonica is, it will likely be constructed virtually the same. All harmonicas have the same basic parts, and we talked about those earlier. You need to understand each part to know how to care for the instrument.

2. Using It Properly

So many things can get in the way of your harmonica producing top-notch sound. Three primary reasons are particulates (saliva and dust), oxidation, and "overplaying."

The temperature in your playing environment can also affect the harmonica reeds. If it is below 50°F (10°C), the reeds can get locked into place, and to free them off, you need to blow gently into the harmonica to warm them up. You must keep your harmonica warm if you live in a cold region or have cold winters. Don't leave them in cold rooms or your car overnight, even if you played late at night.

3. How You Play It

We start with great passion when we learn to play an instrument like the harmonica. However, this can translate into you blowing a lot of saliva into the instrument, which often happens with reed and wind instruments. The drier you can keep your harmonica, the less likely the reeds will fall victim to oxidation and the longer the instrument will last.

Excessive saliva is par for the course with harmonica playing, but you can minimize it by getting into good maintenance habits before, during, and after you play.

The technique you play with determines how much air you blow into the reeds. Regarding your playing intensity, think of it in terms of being a singer. When you have a good posture and play from your diaphragm – breathing deeply but at a normal pace – your tone will improve, as will the health of your harmonica reeds. This is because you don't blow too much saliva into the reeds, and it also prevents the risk of overblowing, which is when you play at such a high pressure, the reeds can become untuned or fail completely. This is common with self-taught and beginner players.

You can also avoid overblowing by using the right embouchure, which depends on which notes you are playing. This comes down to technique, which has mostly been covered in this guide already.

Another simple way is to get into the habit of swallowing your saliva whenever possible. This stops too much piling up in your mouth and entering your harmonica reeds. That said, you should make sure your harmonica is clean when you draw from it and swallow your saliva. We'll talk about cleaning later.

4. A Clean Mouth

It doesn't matter whether you are playing at home, in a large venue, or down the pub, you can enjoy a drink while you play. However, you should also keep water on hand to rinse your mouth, that way, you won't blow some of your drink into the harmonica! It only takes a few micro drops to mess up your reeds or block the holes.

Obviously, it goes the same for food, too. Generally, the cleaner your mouth, the cleaner your harmonica.

5. Good Habits When You Have Finished Playing

To remove some saliva from the reeds and comb, tap your harmonica gently on the palm of your hand, mouthpiece down, when you are finished playing. This will knock out any excess particles.

If you store your harmonica in a case, keep it open for a while after placing the instrument in it. That way, some of the moisture can dry out.

If you use a chromatic harmonica, you can place it, mouthpiece down, in a shallow container of water – do not allow the comb to become wet, only the mouthpiece. Alternatively, allow a little water to drip through the slide assembly. Do one of these before you play and after to wash out saliva, and so the slide doesn't stick to the rest of the harmonica parts.

Cleaning and Maintaining Your Harmonica

No matter how much effort you put into keeping your harmonica in a clean, working order, the time will come when it shows signs of needing to be serviced. It might be that its tuning or playing sound is compromised, or you can see residue on the harmonica comb. You might even get a strange smell coming from it. One of the common issues on a chromatic harmonica is that the slider can become sluggish or even jammed. As I said earlier, most issues can easily be fixed with some simple steps.

The Outer Parts

To keep the mouthpiece of your harmonica clean, use a proper harmonica cleaning spray and a soft cloth to wipe it. If you get the right spray, it will disinfect and clean the mouthpiece while giving it a good shine.

If you want to do a deeper clean, you will need to take the harmonica apart. This must be done carefully, and depending on the make and model of your instrument, you might be able to get a proper maintenance kit. These usually have some good tools to help you keep your harmonica in good shape and could save you from spending money on parts or repairs later or even a new instrument. However, you don't need a kit, you can use a screwdriver that fits your harmonica.

Sit somewhere well-lit with plenty of space and a flat top to work on.

If you have a diatonic harmonica, you can skip this next section.

Cleaning the Slide Assembly and Mouthpiece

As stated at the start of this chapter, chromatic harmonicas often suffer from jammed sliders. This is usually because too much saliva is in there, gluing the parts of the slide assembly together and stopping them from working. You should clean the slide assembly regularly to stop this from happening. However, ensure that the cover plates are screwed on before taking the mouthpiece apart. This will stop unequal pressure from warping the comb.

Usually, there are two more screws on each side of the mouthpiece. Gently unscrew these to reveal rubber bumpers on the ends of the screws. They must stay on the screws and be kept somewhere safe, as they are small enough to be lost easily.

By now, you should have about three or four pieces of your harmonica: the slider and button, the mouthpiece, and the backing plate that fits between the front of the comb and the slider. Depending on the harmonica model, you might find a flange between the slider and mouthpiece, or it might be integrated into the mouthpiece. A very important tip is to note the order of each part in relation to each other regarding orientation and order. Take a photo, or give each piece a number – use a small square of masking tape for each piece. You'll thank yourself when it comes to putting it all back together.

You can now wipe all the parts clean. Wipe the slider with a very thin coat of slider oil, but not too much. Excess oil can slip onto the valves and reeds of your harmonica, making them stick. You won't be able to play your harmonica if this happens.

Now, you can put the slide package back together. Because all harmonica models are different, I can only give you general instructions. Generally, you should ensure all the pieces are aligned on the comb. This ensures that your newly assembled harmonica will be airtight. If you own a Seydel or Chromonic harmonica, the backing plate and flange can be put together to form a chamber; this is where the slider will slide. Slide the slider in and place the whole lot between the comb and the mouthpiece.

When you put all the pieces on top of the comb, carefully ensure that the outside of the spring is inside the slider hole;

this allows your slider to go back into the right place when you press it.

When you screw the mouthpiece back on, make sure you stop when you feel strong resistance and go to the other side. Alternate to keep equal pressure on each side. If one side is put under too much pressure, your slider will become blocked, and if it is left like this for too long, your mouthpiece could warp.

You can do this procedure as often as needed, depending on how often you play or if your slider becomes jammed. The more you do it, the easier it will get.

Reed Plates, Reeds, Comb, and Cover

When you first open your harmonica up, it can be a little frightening. After all, you don't want to damage or lose any of it. However, the time will come when you need to do it to get at the reeds. Honestly, the more you do it, the more satisfying the job is, so long as you use the right tools and follow the instructions carefully.

The first step is to remove the cover plates by unscrewing them on each side. Some will have four screws, and some have two. Once you have removed the cover plates, you may find dried skin and saliva inside them that you can wipe off with a cleaning spray and soft cloth. Alternatively, use a soft toothbrush and warm water. Take care not to lose the screws, as they are very small. Keep a container beside you when you do this, or even better, a small magnetic tray. Also, note where each screw was when you took it out, that way, they all go back to the right place.

With your harmonica open, your next job is to take the reed plates off the comb. This is a delicate job. The reeds are incredibly vulnerable and sensitive and produce the tuning and tone in your harmonica. You can change the tuning and tone when you handle these roughly or make poor adjustments. For this reason, your harmonica should be kept vertical and not leaned to one side. It also should not rest on its cover plates. Keeping it vertical ensures that the reed plates are not put under any pressure. Some harmonica manufacturers will ask you to follow the old policy of "if it ain't broke, don't fix it," meaning there's no need to clean the reeds if your harmonica is playing well.

You can start by leaving the reed plates and comb screwed together and rinsing them under warm water to remove the saliva. However, you should only do this if there are no wind savers or valves in your harmonica. You will normally find these on chromatic instruments, but some diatonic ones do have them. This is also a good step if your combs are sealed or made of metal; wooden combs then do swell if they haven't been sealed.

Next, unscrew the reed plates. Loosen all the screws a little first, then unscrew them all fully, ensuring you don't place undue pressure on the plate. You should end up with the two reed plates, the comb, and the screws. Again, ensure to note which hole each screw comes from and keep them in the right order within your container.

Now you can clean the reed plates and comb.

If you have a maintenance kit, use the reed-lifting tool to scrape the comb gently to remove residue. Make sure you do not damage the metal or wood. Once done, you can use a soft toothbrush to graze the comb and between its teeth.

25. Use the reed-lifting tool to scrape the comb gently to remove residue. Source: https://www.wikihow.com/images/thumb/6/6e/Clean-a-Harmonica-Step-8-Version-2.jpg/v4-460px-Clean-a-Harmonica-Step-8-Version-2.jpg.webp

I must urge caution when handling the reed plates. Hold them at the edges and use the lifting tool to lift each reed individually and allow it to bounce back. This will remove anything stuck to the edge that might stop them from working as they should.

You can use a soft cloth to wipe the reed plate edges but do not use a cloth or brush to clean the reeds or reed slots.

If your harmonica has valves, you can clean them of any residue that might be stuck to them. Make sure everything is dry, and lift the valve using a slim piece of plastic or a needle.

Insert a damp piece of paper softly between the valve and hole – a damp coffee filter will do the job. Rub the valve gently on the paper to clean the residue off.

You can also soak the reed plates in a solution of lukewarm water and white vinegar for 20 minutes before you scrape the residue off. Remember, this can only be done with harmonicas that don't have valves. If you do soak the plates, rinse them in lukewarm water and dab them dry carefully – do NOT rub them.

Now all your harmonica parts are clean and dry, you can put the instrument back together.

First, screw the reed plates carefully onto the comb, tightening the screw slowly and equally so as not to put unequal pressure on the plate. As soon as you feel strong resistance, stop turning the screws. This is crucial because if you under or over-tighten the screws, the reed plate may warp, and your harmonica won't be airtight. It will also not be in tune because the reeds won't be aligned.

Now the cover plates may be screwed back on, again making sure not to put unequal pressure on any part. Test each hole to ensure they all play correctly, and try the slider to ensure it works, too.

As you disassemble your harmonica, you will see just how delicate it is. It can also be quite temperamental because the smallest variable, especially preventable ones, can change how it works. Prevention is always better than cure, and regular maintenance is better than having to do serious repairs to your harmonica or, worse, having to replace it.

Hopefully, the tips in this chapter will help you keep your harmonica clean and maintained so you can enjoy playing it for many years to come.

Conclusion

Obviously, you are interested in learning how to play the harmonica, and I hope I have been able to help you with the basics.

This guide covered everything you need to know.

Chapter 1 discussed where the harmonica originated – it is very old – and the main types of harmonica you will likely use. We also looked at the different parts of the harmonica and finished with the definitions of the most common terms and phrases you will hear.

Chapter 2 discussed how to choose the right harmonica. You learned about basic positions and keys, a technique called bending, and got a look at the harmonica positions chart.

Chapter 3 delved into how to hold your harmonica and play it. We looked at your posture, how to position your hands, lips, and mouth, and how to breathe properly and included some breathing exercises to help you.

Chapter 4 looked at techniques such as tongue blocking and how to play single notes. We also determined the benefits that tongue blocking offers, including the ability to play missing notes.

Chapter 5 was about simple melodies. It looked at how to read harmonica music, change holes and your breath, and improve your listening skills, which are important for learning to play the harmonica. This chapter also provided some simple melodies to practice.

Chapter 6 was all about chords, chord progressions, and scales, which are important as they help you advance from playing simple notes to chords and melodies.

Chapter 7 looked at two advanced techniques crucial to your learning journey: vibrato and tremolo. Learning these allows you to take your music to the next level, injecting interest and expression and allowing your audience to understand what you are trying to say with your harmonica.

Chapter 8 provided tips on improvisation and jamming, while Chapter 9 discussed the equipment needed and some useful tips on playing your harmonica amplified. The last chapter, chapter 10 covered how to clean, maintain, and care for your harmonica so you can play it for years to come.

This has been an in-depth guide, and there is a lot of information for you to take in. My advice is to take it one chapter at a time. After mastering it, take a break before moving on to the next chapter.

If you found my guide useful and enjoyed it, please leave a review for me and potential readers.

References

10 Easy Harmonica Songs (& How to Play Them) | Beginner Harmonica Lesson & Harp Tabs. (2023, May 2). LearnTheHarmonica. https://www.learntheharmonica.com/post/10-easy-harmonica-songs-beginner-harmonica-lesson-tabs

Allen, J. P. (2010, April 15). *How to Buy the Right Harmonica – What Really Matters.* Harmonica.com. https://www.harmonica.com/things-you-need-to-know-before-buying-harmonica/

Breathing Exercises for Harmonica Players. (n.d.). Dummies. https://www.dummies.com/article/academics-the-arts/music/instruments/harmonica/breathing-exercises-for-harmonica-players-146671/

Derhgawen, A. (2009, June 2). *Harmonica Keys and Positions Explained – Everything You Need to Understand Harmonica Keys.* Harmonica.com. https://www.harmonica.com/harmonica-keys-positions/

Harmonica Bending For Beginners. (2021, October 19). LearnTheHarmonica.

https://www.learntheharmonica.com/post/harmonica-bending-for-beginners

Harmonica History | Harmonicatunes. (n.d.). https://harmonicatunes.com/harmonica-history/#:~:text=and%20beautiful%20music.-

Harmonica Notes. (n.d.). PlayMusic123.com. https://www.playmusic123.com/blogs/news/harmonica-notes

Harmonica Notes: the easy guide to harmonica note layout. (2020, December 10). LearnTheHarmonica. https://www.learntheharmonica.com/post/harmonica-notes-easy-guide-layout

Harmonica Scales in 1st, 2nd, 3rd Positions | Major, Minor and Blues. (2022, January 25). LearnTheHarmonica. https://www.learntheharmonica.com/post/harmonica-scales-1st-2nd-3rd-positions

How to Bend Harmonica – For Beginners. (2020, December 16). Harmonica.com. https://www.harmonica.com/how-to-bend-harmonica/

How To Breathe When Playing Harmonica. (n.d.). TheMusicStand.ca. https://www.themusicstand.ca/blogs/htp-harmonica/breathe

How to care for your Harmonica | Eagle Music Harmonica Maintenance Guide. (n.d.). Www.eaglemusicshop.com. https://www.eaglemusicshop.com/harmonicas/harmonica-advice/how-to-care-for-your-harmonica

How to Hold a Harmonica. (n.d.). Musicalinstrumentguide.com. https://musicalinstrumentguide.com/how-to-hold-a-harmonica/

How to Move from One Note to the Next on the Harmonica. (n.d.). Dummies. https://www.dummies.com/article/academics-the-arts/music/instruments/harmonica/how-to-move-from-one-note-to-the-next-on-the-harmonica-146637/

How to Project Your Harmonica Sound with Your Hands. (n.d.). Dummies. https://www.dummies.com/article/academics-the-arts/music/instruments/harmonica/how-to-project-your-harmonica-sound-with-your-hands-146631/

Luke. (2019, August 30). *How to Play Harmonica Chords – For Beginners.* Harmonica.com. https://www.harmonica.com/harmonica-chords/

Luke. (2022, March 22). *Exploring the 3 Types of Harmonica – A Beginner's Guide.* Harmonica.com. https://www.harmonica.com/exploring-the-3-types-of-harmonica/

Parts of a Harmonica: Anatomy Explained | Hello Music Theory. (2021, November 11). https://hellomusictheory.com/learn/parts-of-the-harmonica/

Peters, J. (2023a, February 2). *How to Read Harmonica Tab: An Essential Guide for All Harmonica Players.* Country Instruments. https://countryinstruments.com/how-to-read-harmonica-tab/

Peters, J. (2023b, February 3). *Learn How to Play Single Notes on Harmonica: A Step-by-Step Guide.* Country Instruments. https://countryinstruments.com/how-to-play-single-notes-on-harmonica/

Play Single Notes on Harmonica, 2 Ways to Master Fast. (2023, March 25). Harmonicaforall.com. https://harmonicaforall.com/blues-harmonica/play-single-notes-on-harmonica-2/

Playing Chords With Your Harmonica. (n.d.). TheMusicStand.ca. https://www.themusicstand.ca/blogs/htp-harmonica/chords

Prestidge, J. (2020, January 23). *Harmonica Positions Explained.* The Harmonica Company. https://theharmonicacompany.com/blog/harmonica-positions-explained/

The Beginner's Guide to Harmonicas for Curious Newbies. (2017, September 4). E-Home Recording Studio. https://ehomerecordingstudio.com/best-harmonicas/

What it is Harmonica and how to play it | Simplifying Theory. (n.d.). https://www.simplifyingtheory.com/what-is-harmonica-how-to-play-it/

Printed in Great Britain
by Amazon